INVESTIGATING NATURE
THROUGH OUTDOOR PROJECTS

Illustrations by
      Jill Bewley
      Irene Brady
      Natalie Geiger
      Marshall Hasbrouck
      Julian LaCalle

Investigating Nature Through Outdoor Projects

36 strategies for turning the natural environment into your own laboratory

VINSON BROWN

STACKPOLE BOOKS

Published by
STACKPOLE BOOKS
Cameron and Kelker Streets
P. O. Box 1831
Harrisburg, PA 17105

Printed in the U.S.A.

Library of Congress Cataloging in Publication Data
Brown, Vinson, 1912-
Investigating nature through outdoor projects.

Bibliography: p.
Includes index.
1. Biology--Field work. I. Title.
QH318.5.B7   1983   574.0723   82-19660
ISBN 0-8117-2213-9 (pbk.)

372.3

*To my new and lovely daughter by marriage,
Sheila Brown, in deep appreciation of her good
character and her love for and interest in the
natural world around her.*

Contents

Introduction   9

ADVENTURES WITH MAMMALS

1 Full-Moon Rabbit Dance   13
2 Skunk Antics   15
3 Using Dummy Animals to Attract Others   19

ADVENTURES WITH BIRDS

4 Backyard Birds   29
5 Special Methods for Observing Birds   49

ADVENTURES WITH REPTILES

6 Snakes   57
7 Lizards   65
8 Turtles and Tortoises   73

ADVENTURES WITH INSECTS AND SPIDERS

9   Capturing and Keeping Live Insects   81
10 The Incredible Ants   99
11 Amazing Antlions   109
12 Testing the Strength of Insects   115
13 How They Can Jump!   119
14 Wonderful Spiders and Their Webs   123

ADVENTURES IN DIFFERENT HABITATS

15 Tracking and Trail Finding   141
16 Tree-Dwelling Mammals, Reptiles, Amphibians, and Insects   151
17 Succession of Plants and Animals   155
18 Burrowing Animals   165
19 Ponds, Streams, and Freshwater Aquariums   173
20 Tide Pools and Saltwater Aquariums   187
21 Denizens of the Desert Night   203
22 Exploring Swamp Life in a Muskrat Nest Blind   215

ADVENTURES WITH PLANTS

23 Protected Wild Garden   223
24 Special Herb Garden   233

References   243

Index   249

Introduction

A THRILL IS defined in the dictionary as something that causes "sharply exhilarating excitement" or that makes one "shiver or tingle with excitement." I believe every one of the suggested projects in this book can give you such a thrill if you approach it with the idea of discovering something new and interesting that gives you the feeling of sudden discovery or enlightened knowledge. Too many people, however, go through life without such thrills because their senses are deadened. Somewhere along the line they have lost that childlike interest in new things, new ideas, and new experiences that make all of life a thrilling experience. I hope you will be one of those who are awakened to the adventures that can be found in the out-of-doors.

Many projects in this book can help train you to be more aware of the world around you, and to use that awareness to grow in sensitivity and knowledge until you can take your place among the true heroes of life who have dedicated themselves to knowing, finding, and making a better and more interesting world. Too many people reach a certain age and stop growing. They have a job, a family, friends, a home, a car, and a TV; they think that is all there is to life. Somehow they have died and do not know it. Life must stay alive and be investigated for its thrills if we are to truly live. And there are many many thrills of living to be found in the out-of-doors.

You can learn from this book how to be an amateur naturalist, but to become a professional naturalist takes long training. As you follow the suggestions in this book, realize that you are only on a beginning trail in your learning, and that a whole universe of new discoveries stretches before you yet unexplored or not truly learned about. If you keep this wide-open feeling of always being on the brink of new discoveries, then you will be on the way to becoming a real naturalist, for no one can claim to be a naturalist who does not continually have a seeking, exploring, and thrilling mind. Keeping a notebook handy and writing down the new sights, new sounds, new experiences you find is a way to constantly grow in knowledge and to hold that knowledge in your records.

I remember many great thrills in my life that have come through the sudden discovery of what I never knew before. There was the Bell bird, whose exquisite song in the Panama mountain jungle struck my heart, indeed my whole being, with a sudden knowledge of something beyond all other music I had ever heard. There was an equal feeling of meeting incomparable visual beauty recently when I suddenly came on a California mountain kingsnake, coiled by a rotting log, in all its loveliness of crimson, golden, and glittering black bands on a supple body that vanished like lightning under a bush. There was an equal, but very different, thrill when I discovered the huge, funny-looking worm called "A Fat Innkeeper" in the mud of Bodega Bay on the Pacific Coast. What a strange-looking creature! What amazing and amusing animals came to live in his or her "inn!"

You too, I hope, will use this book to find such thrills and increase your knowledge. Your whole family, if you have one, will learn too, and perhaps your neighbors. It is a way to grow in life and become a more complete and well-balanced human being, aware of your surroundings and their meanings as never before. Try some of these projects and live as you never have lived! But keep your eyes and ears open, all your senses alert. Learn to be a naturalist.

ADVENTURES WITH MAMMALS

1

Full-Moon Rabbit Dance

COTTONTAIL RABBITS OFTEN love to dance together on full-moon nights (or sometimes dawns) in summer, and it is a wondrous and funny sight to see. You must find by daylight a place where they dance. This is usually in a fairly open woods but right near a large thicket of blackberries or other thorn-armed bramble bushes in which the rabbits can escape from their enemies. You will see many rabbit droppings there in a kind of circle and places where they have thumped the ground bare.

If you look closely, you will see trails leading to this place and the tracks of rabbits in places in the trails where there is loose dirt or mud. You may also find rabbit fur caught on the brambles where rabbits have passed. All these are helpful signs that this may be a rabbit dancing circle.

To prepare for the evening, rub your body and clothes with the leaves of a strong-smelling plant like honeysuckle, bay, or sagebrush and wear dark clothes. Use a dark-colored tarp or cloth to form a plain upside-down V tent, in which you can lie full-length to watch the rabbits from a distance of about thirty to forty feet. You can bring blankets or sleeping bags and lie in or on these while watching the rabbits.

Be sure to lie perfectly still where you are in complete darkness, so the rabbits will not know you are there. Use binoculars if you have them. But do not let the moonlight touch and flash on the lenses.

At first, only a few rabbits will probably come to make sure everything is all right, then more and more until perhaps a couple of dozen begin to jump and dance. You can observe how they touch noses and communicate if you watch closely, and you will sometimes see how some rabbits will dominate others. As the dance gets under way, the rabbits begin to form several circles. The night gets more and more exciting as the rabbits jump over one another higher and higher, as if to show off their powers. The mad whirling becomes very startling, and the rabbits may get into a literal frenzy of power and excitement. What a rare and wonderful sight to see!

You may have a good chance to see other animals, too, as the dance usually ends when a dog, wildcat, fox, coyote, or great-horned owl suddenly attacks out of the dark and seizes one of the rabbits. What a tremendous squealing and thumping of many feet as the rabbits jump away and dive into the bramble bushes as quickly as they can, while the captured rabbit is carried off by its enemy!

The whole adventure gives you a thrilling look into the life of the night.

Another time you could sprinkle a white powder on the ground around the outer circumference of the dance area. In the morning you can discover from tracks that are left what kinds of animals came to watch the dance or to hunt a rabbit.

Why do rabbits have this dance? Perhaps for exactly the same reasons that young people come together to dance on a Saturday night—for fun and frolic and girl-meeting-boy. Another possibility is that the dance is a kind of rabbit worship of the full moon, as if they are paying their respects to it. When you see the rabbits dance (and I am not going to guarantee you will ever see it, because the rabbits may be too shy), I hope you watch carefully and see if you can think of other meanings why they come together for such gymnastics.

2

Skunk Antics

SKUNKS ARE SLOW-MOVING animals and cannot or will not run as fast as you can run. They will not attack you with their strong- and bad-smelling scent glands which throw out a poisonous spray unless they are fairly sure you are about to attack them.* I have followed one of these funny animals for hours in the night, using a flashlight covered with red plastic, and never had the slightest need to be afraid because I always kept a safe distance of at least fifteen feet away from it. The red light enabled me to see the skunk plainly but did not bother the skunk as a white light would.

You, too, can do this. Walk quietly in soft-soled shoes until the skunk becomes used to your silent following of it and begins to act normally. By wearing dark clothes and rubbing them with a strong-smelling plant like honeysuckle or sagebrush, you can reduce the skunk's awareness of your presence. Soon the skunk will naturally stop and sniff at a rock or log or board that is on the ground and turn it over to

---

*There may be a *rare* chance that a skunk is rabid. If it tries to attack you without provocation, get away from it quickly and call the police, animal shelter, or pound. Since you can outrun it, do not be afraid.

see if there are any interesting creatures underneath. Grubs, worms, ants are all grabbed and stuffed in its mouth. If it uncovers a mouse nest, what excitement there is! The skunk grabs as fast as it can for the baby mice while the mama mouse seizes the babies with her teeth and quickly drags a few away to safety in a new underground hole.

Something drastic happens when a skunk is attacked by a dog or other larger animals. If the skunk is a striped skunk, it lifts its great plumed tail and releases almost instantly a cloud of nasty-smelling gas right into the dog's face. The dog immediately retreats yelping and trying desperately to rub its face into the dirt and get that awful stuff off! If the skunk is a small spotted skunk, it stands up suddenly on its front feet, lifting its rear end high and lets go a terrific whiff of stink at the enemy. Why does this smaller skunk do this? Possibly because of its small size it wants to get its gas-throwing end up as high as possible to throw the bad-smelling stuff farther. Another possibility is that it wants to raise its warning white-tipped tail, which has hairs sticking out stiffly, as high as possible above the bushes or grasses so that the attacking animal or man knows immediately *this is a skunk!*

You can test the intelligence of a skunk and have fun watching it by building a simple maze in your backyard if skunks come there at night, or somewhere else you can visit easily if they do not. Use wire netting about three feet high or old plyboards of the same height and make a maze like that shown in Figure 2–1. Because skunks are great carrion eaters, they will be attracted by animal remains which you can get from a butcher and place in the center of your maze. Watch with red lights as the skunk enters the maze to find the food it smells. Be very quiet and use a timer to see how long it takes the skunk to reach the food. Draw a diagram of the maze, make copies, and trace with a colored pen or pencil the routes followed by the skunk each time it goes through the maze. This, along with the time taken, will give you a truly scientific record of the skunk's intelligence, as well as an interesting and fun-filled night. One thing I anticipate you will discover is that skunks learn a maze at different speeds—a few very quickly, others slower.

If you ever find a mother skunk with her kits following solemnly and respectfully behind her, you are in for the best thrill of all. They may be well mannered for a while, but wait until they find a mouse nest or termite nest. Then watch the fireworks! Once I watched five funny little skunk kittens when they encountered a yellow-jacket nest in the night. Wow! The whole family broke up for most of the evening after that, with mama rushing around trying to find her lost kits!

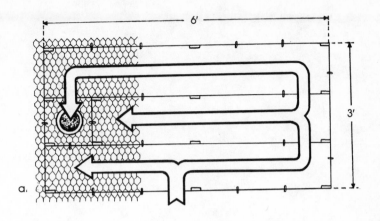

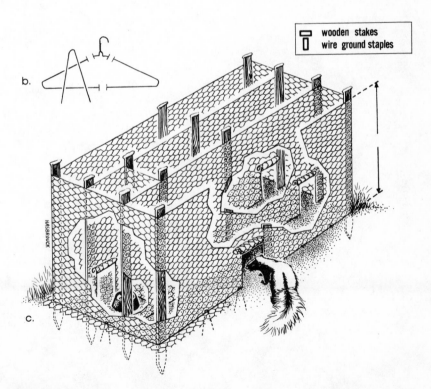

Figure 2–1. Skunk maze. (*a*) Maze diagram showing placement of wooden stakes and wire ground staples. (*b*) How to cut wire ground staples from a wire coat hanger. (*c*) Cutaway drawing of completed skunk maze.

3

Using Dummy Animals to Attract Others

ALMOST ALL HUNTING animals depend upon watching the movements of their prey to see how to catch them, and almost all hunted animals, such as mice and rats and rabbits, depend either on speed or absolute stillness and camouflage to escape their enemies. Also, most mammals, especially in the spring and summer, have territories that they guard from others of the same species, particularly when they are raising their young. Thus, you can use dummy animals to attract predators so you can see how they hunt or to attract other individuals of the same species who become angry because they think your dummy animal is invading their territory. In these and other actions that may occur you can learn a lot about animal habits with your dummies.

EQUIPMENT NEEDED

How to make a dummy rabbit or mouse is shown in the accompanying pictures. The dummy should be made as realistic as possible, and have the correct colors for each species you might want to show (see Figures 3–1 and 3–2). Colors can be learned from the books listed in the suggested references of this book, which are easily obtained from libraries. The more accurate your animal dummy appears, the more likely it is to attract either an enemy or a friend or a rival. How to place these animals on a stump or other likely place where they are able to attract visitors is shown in Figure 3–3. These illustrations also show how to fix dummies with almost invisible fish lines so you can make them move realistically. It is these movements that almost immediately attract a predator. If you get a special whistle or make one with grass blades (Figure 3–4), you will also be able to make actual sounds similar to the animal sounds and attract visitors even more quickly.

To make a sound, put a large flat grass blade to your lips, wet it with your tongue, and then hold it there tightly while blowing against the blade. It takes practice to make this work and to get a squeaking noise, so do not be discouraged if you get nothing at first. Perhaps a friend who knows how might show you how to master the sound.

The fish lines are used to push or pull the dummy mouse, rabbit, or woodrat back and forth across the stump's flat top until something happens. Your own position should be behind a bush or tree at least twenty, and preferably more, feet away.

WHAT YOU CAN EXPECT TO HAPPEN

Several animals are likely to come to a movable mouse or rabbit on a stump in a woods clearing and attempt to kill and eat it: a coyote or fox would probably dash at the dummy from a hiding place behind a bush; a weasel would move low down and hidden in the grass, but come swiftly; a skunk would probably come slowly and be puzzled as to why the dumb mouse or rabbit did not run away; a ring-tailed cat would come gracefully and lightly leaping from behind the animal to strike from the rear; and a bear (in mountain woods) would be more puzzled than even the skunk and would probably try to sneak up on it slowly.

Animals that would come to play, fight for territory, court or act as rivals would probably be of the same species as the dummy. They would come, but might be disgusted when they discovered it was a dummy! Any observations should be recorded in a notebook (see my *Amateur Naturalists Diary*, published by Prentice-Hall), and also recorded in photographs. Your notes will be much more valuable to

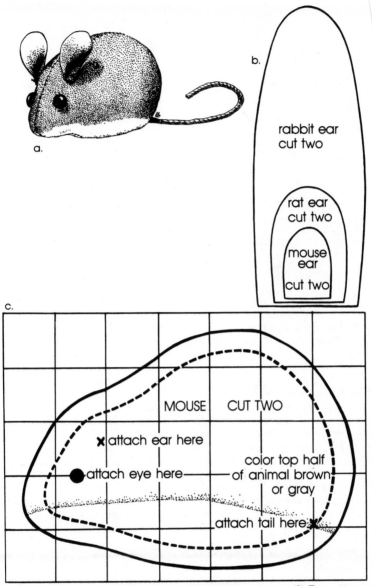

b.

rabbit ear
cut two

rat ear
cut two

mouse
ear
cut two

a.

c.

MOUSE CUT TWO

X attach ear here

● attach eye here

color top half
of animal brown
or gray

attach tail here **X**

Figure 3–1. Dummy mouse pattern. (*a*) **Completed dummy mouse.** (*b*) **Ear patterns. Do not enlarge. Color cloth before cutting.** (*c*) **Pattern for mouse. To enlarge, draw pattern on grid with 1 inch squares. To enlarge for rat, use grid with 1⅛ inch squares. To enlarge for rabbit, use grid with 1½ inch squares. Supplies needed: cloth or felt (8 inches square for mouse, 9 inches square for rat, 12 inches square for rabbit); needle; 5–10 pins; scissors; felt tip marker, brown or gray; stuffing; shiny black beads or buttons; thread, gray or brown; string, 4 to 8 inches (or cotton ball for rabbit).**

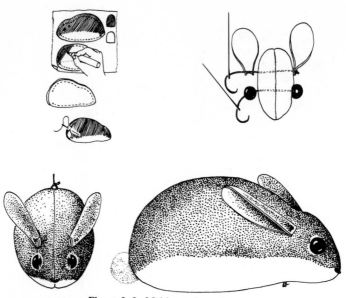

Figure 3–2. Making a dummy mouse.

1. **Supplies:** Gather all supplies to be used. See Figure 3–1. Read instructions all the way through before beginning.

2. **Pattern:** Make mouse, rat, or rabbit pattern by transferring outline to larger grid on paper.

3. **Cloth:** On cloth which is the lightest color on the animal (white if animal has white belly, or gray if belly is gray), draw the pattern. Make two body outlines (one facing left and one facing right) and two ear outlines.

4. **Markings:** Before cutting, color animal with felt tip marker. See pattern to find where color usually begins on side of animal. Color ears. Color string if making mouse or rat. Cut out body and ears.

5. **Pin body parts together with colored sides facing each other. Sew around edge, about ¼ inch in from perimeter, leaving 1 inch unsewed at rear of mouse. Turn inside out.

6. **Stuff body, turn edges of opening inside, and finish sewing body.

7. **Ears:** Double ear over with brown side out. Pass needle through base of ear as shown. Continue pushing needle through head at point marked with an X on animal's head. Pass needle through base of second ear, pull tight, and secure.

8. **Eyes:** Sew bead or button to head as you did for the ears. Position bead as marked with black circle on head of animal pattern.

9. **Tail:** Sew one end of string to body at point marked with an X on rear end of animal pattern. Dummy is finished.

10. **Rat or rabbit:** Rat's tail should be 6 inches long and made from heavy ¼ inch string or cord. Rabbit's tail is a cotton puff sewed on at the rear X. It would be best to make the rabbit's ears from felt to make them stiff enough to be realistic. A rabbit's ears are aimed to the back, with the opening facing down to keep out rain. Color or stitch a nose on your dummy if you want.

Figure 3–3. Mounting movable dummy mouse on a stump. (*a*) Attach heavy wire between two trees or bushes; string a plastic ring onto wire before attaching the ends. (*b*) Attach one end of fishing line to dummy, other end to center ring. (*c*) Tie two lengths of fishing line to ring and run ends to blind. Pull strings from blind to make dummy move.

yourself and to others, especially scientists, if you do an accurate job. You will have more success watching for any or all these animals in the moonlight or even on dark nights, using a red flashlight, than during the day, as most are night hunters.

The following birds would be most likely to attack your dummy in the nighttime: a great-horned owl, huge in size, coming in low and swiftly on silent wings, probably tearing your dummy to pieces before you could save it; a barn owl, likely to come like a white ghost in more open areas such as a field or barnyard; a screech owl, coming secretly from bush to bush because it is afraid of the horned owl, and then seizing a mouse, but likely to leave a rabbit alone; and a saw-whet owl, also grabbing only a mouse.

Daytime bird attackers of both mouse and rabbit would be a red-tailed hawk, diving down from high in the sky and screaming his territorial rights when he seizes the prey; a red-shouldered hawk (Pacific

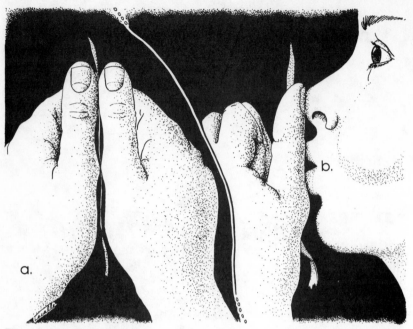

Figure 3–4. Grass blade squeaker. (*a*) Hold grass blade stretched tightly between thumbs. (*b*) Blow hard between knuckles.

Coast and eastern North America), watching from a treetop and then diving down to seize his dinner; a short-eared owl, more likely to attack in early morning or evening in dusky light, coming in very low to the ground and swerving suddenly to grab its prey; a golden eagle, so rare that you might see this magnificent bird whistling down from high in the sky to seize your rabbit (it would scorn a mouse!) only once in a lifetime; and a marsh-hawk, who would wing in low and beautifully poised for a sudden drop on its prey, or a side-to-side harrying.

Usually, eaters of only the mouse would be (in desert areas) road-runners, running up at high speed to leap suddenly for the prey, and crows and ravens, swooping from the sky but astonished if the mouse did not disappear. In the West, the light-colored Swainson's hawk might appear out of the sun so the mouse would not see it, or a burrowing owl, who hunts mostly by day in dry country, might leap up from its hiding place on a hillock and swirl over in a kind of sideways attack meant to befuddle its prey.

A few very large snakes, such as a big gopher snake, racer, or rattlesnake, will attack a rabbit, the rattlesnake moving very slowly and striking from hiding when the rabbit passes by, and then waiting until the poison takes effect. The gopher snake seizes the rabbit with its teeth, after sneaking up, but then raps its body around it to constrict it. Smaller snakes prefer mice. A whip-snake, for example, dashes up at high speed and bites to kill, but a rubber boa of the Far West comes at night to silently constrict its prey. Watch any snake closely, for different kinds attack differently.

HOW TO SET UP

It is extremely vital for you to be hidden in a good place, such as thick brush, behind rocks, or in a blind (Figure 3–5) where you can be fairly certain you cannot be seen by the animals or birds that come to your decoys. You must also sit or lie still and not talk if you have a partner with you, though it may be all right to whisper very softly. Your clothes should be of colors that camouflage you in brush, usually brown mottled with gray, or light tan (if you are in desert country. Binoculars or field glasses of 7-power or higher will bring the creatures close to you.

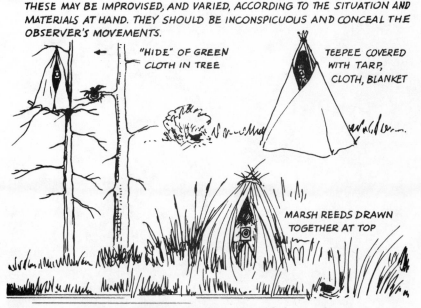

THESE MAY BE IMPROVISED, AND VARIED, ACCORDING TO THE SITUATION AND MATERIALS AT HAND. THEY SHOULD BE INCONSPICUOUS AND CONCEAL THE OBSERVER'S MOVEMENTS.

"HIDE" OF GREEN CLOTH IN TREE

TEEPEE COVERED WITH TARP, CLOTH, BLANKET

MARSH REEDS DRAWN TOGETHER AT TOP

Figure 3–5. Blinds for bird observation and photography.

ADVENTURES WITH BIRDS

4

Backyard Birds

IT IS DELIGHTFUL to have birds singing in your backyard or gardens, or even to lure them to a nearby park. It is also exciting to follow their adventures and that of other animals and creatures that will come to such places. To begin, you need to express love and friendship toward these creatures in your heart and mind, movements and activities, so that eventually they will come to trust you. One person reported that over five hundred birds visited her home and gardens in a single month because she had made her place so attractive to them! Whole books have been written about how to do this, but I am going to tell you how in a few pages with a few vital drawings; hopefully, this will inspire you to create unique things yourself to attract birds and animals. Also get from the library some of the books mentioned in the references.

CREATING BIRD HABITATS

There are certain plants that attract birds and butterflies as well as other creatures. But never crowd your plants and trees so they cut out too much sunlight because most birds, particularly song birds, like to have lighted open areas.

Many kinds of berry bushes, but not the kind that have poisonous berries, attract birds. Maples, oaks, willows, cottonwoods, and walnuts are attractive trees. Flowers with deep-throated corollas and bright red, yellow, or orange colors especially attract hummingbirds and bumblebees. Herbs like the clovers, violets, lilies, orchids, roses, mustards, gilias, and wild peas attract insects, which in turn attract birds. One of the adventures you can do is to try many plants and learn from experience which attract the birds, then concentrate on them.

Every fall it is wise to build a brush pile in your garden where birds can find hiding places from enemies and where they can get out of the rain, wind, or snow. Pile up large branches first and then small branches on top of these to a height of five or six feet. Place plenty of fir boughs on top if you have them and add your Christmas tree later to the top of the pile.

Once you have plants around on your property there is nothing like water to attract birds. Besides liking to drink water without having to go too far for it, birds love to take baths. Pools for drinking and bathing should be shallow, sloping gradually from one to five or six inches deep. Pans supported by wood so they are above the general ground level are one way; better still is to have a pool (possibly cement) set on a central pole six or more feet above ground so cats cannot get at the birds too easily. If you can hang a hose or even a large bucket full of water in a tree above the pool and let it drip about every fifteen to twenty seconds, this will attract many birds more than anything else. The sound of the dripping water brings them in a hurry.

Birds suffer greatly in winter from the cold and especially from ice and heavy snow. But as long as they get enough food, they can stand intense cold if they can get out of the wind because their rapid body metabolism keeps them warm. Even so, you can often see birds shivering on cold days, and nothing pleases them better than a chance to warm their feet. This you can give them. There are a few kinds of water heaters that can be put into bird baths or pools to keep them warm in winter and greatly help the birds stay alive. The ordinary submersible water heater needs to be connected by a lead-covered waterproof electric cord to the outlet in your house. It should be buried so it's out of the way of digging tools and Rototillers, or it can be extended overhead from some supports. The water heater is set in a pan at least six inches deep, never in a cement bird bath, which may crack; stones or building bricks are put in with it to cover the heater and give a rough bottom for the birds to stand on. Turn on the heater only when the water begins to freeze and leave it on longest during the hardest freezes. About a 75-watt heater is fine as it actually uses only small amounts of electricity. A better heater still is one that is thermostatically controlled to go on when the temperature drops below forty degrees Fahrenheit and to go off when the temperature rises over fifty degrees. You may wish to adjust the heater to increase the temperature. Ask about this at pet stores.

In the spring, a place where dripping or seeping water produces mud is especially helpful to birds that build mud or mud-lined nests such as robins and swallows. A small seep from a faucet placed where there is clayey soil will do the job.

The more you can do to keep birds comfortable the more they will come to visit you and the more insects and other plant pests they will eat, so your garden will continue to grow and give you beautiful flowers plus good fruits or vegetables.

Feeding birds will also make birds your friends and bring them to your garden in quantities. It will, in time, give you and others the great thrill of having a wild bird come and take food from your hand or even from your lips. I remember the wonderful thrill as a child when I visited a bird woman's garden and she showed me how the hummingbirds took honey water from a red-painted pipette in her hand. Then she told me to stand perfectly still, put a pipette in between my lips, and let a hummingbird come and drink its food from my mouth. This elfin bird, so much like a magic fairy in its quick actions, marvelous dives through space, and whizzing wings, made me feel like the greatest of conquerors when it touched my lips with its delicate long bill.

FEEDING PLACES FOR BIRDS

The bird feeders shown in the following pictures are suggested ways to attract birds, but you can also feed them by throwing food scraps on the ground or putting such tidbits on top of a large rock. Feeding birds is particularly important during the cold months of the year, but sometimes it is also vital when nesting birds lose one mate and the single parent that remains is having a hard time getting enough food for the young. Then a feeder with food on it near that nest may save lives. Once you have begun feeding birds in the cold months, do not stop the feeding too soon in the spring, as a cold storm may come in from the north and wipe out a lot of your bird population at a time when they need to be fed most.

The trolley feeder (Figure 4–1, top), is especially important in getting birds to lose their fear of you and become friends with you. You begin with this feeder on its trolley far away from your house where the birds feel perfectly safe, but where they can begin to realize that this food comes from you. Each day you bring the feeder a little closer to your window, until finally the birds are feeding right at your window and can be observed very closely. At such times make no sudden movements so you do not scare them. Tame birds like these will sing when you are quite near them and also let you come near their nests with little fear, especially if you move slowly and carefully and go away if they seem too disturbed. After the trolley feeder has done its job, then you can put a more permanent window shelf-feeder right by the window, and start again with the trolley feeder to tame some other birds for another window.

When you build feeders be sure to leave no rough edges and put roofs on them if you have much rainy weather. Roofs should extend out so that the rain has a hard time getting in. If wind is a problem, put a plastic window along one side and turn this side of the bird feeder towards the wind. Another way to counter the wind is to build a weather vane feeder (Figure 4–1, center), which automatically turns to face away from the wind so the plastic window in the back is always towards the wind.

The experimental bird cafeteria (Figure 4–2) is a way to help you determine which kinds of feed suit the birds best. You can put a different kind of food in each of the trays and then watch carefully from day to day to see which food disappears most quickly. Keep notes on what you see so you can begin to give the birds the more popular foods. One thing I should warn you about is never to mix greasy food, such as the leavings of a chicken dinner, with dry seeds or bread. Some birds will be disturbed by this and not eat at all.

Also, always provide at least two different feeders, and probably two different kinds, so that small birds that are shy and afraid of the larger birds will have a place to come and feed. To make sure the small birds are completely protected from the larger birds, build a feeder that has two open doors for entranceways that are too narrow for the larger

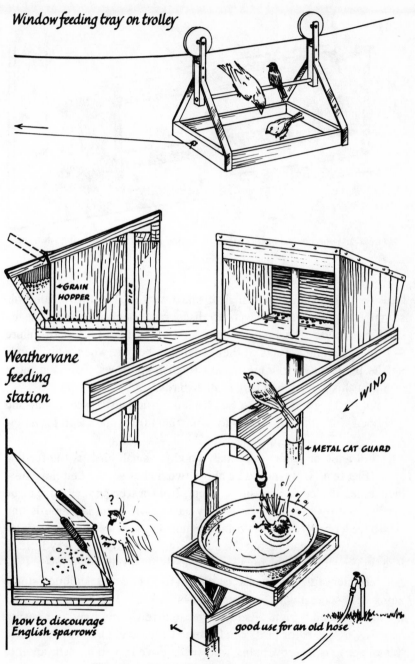

Window feeding tray on trolley

Weathervane
feeding
station

←GRAIN
HOPPER

PIPE

WIND

←METAL CAT GUARD

how to discourage
English sparrows

good use for an old hose

Figure 4–1. Bird feeding and watering stations.

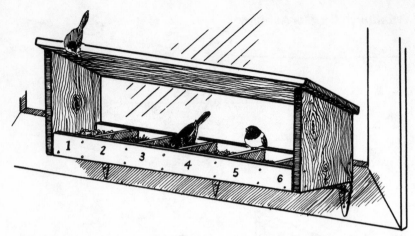

Figure 4–2. Experimental bird cafeteria for testing which foods different birds prefer.

birds to get in. Sometimes English sparrows give the other small birds so much trouble that you want to discourage them from eating in the small bird feeder. This can be done, as shown at the bottom of Figure 4–1, by attaching springs to the feeder that bounce when a bird lands on the platform. For some reason English sparrows are much more afraid of this arrangement than other birds.

All bird feeders need to be cleaned out at least twice a year and scrubbed with soap and water to make them fresh and clean for a new season.

Still another feeder especially good for small birds is the feeding stick (Figure 4–3). It should be about two inches square and have one-inch holes drilled in the sides. Hung from a tree branch, it can be approached by the small birds very easily, while the large birds find such a feeder hard to hang onto and are more frightened by its movements.

Suet, which can be obtained from butcher shops for very little or free, is especially good for the birds early in spring when insects are not very plentiful. It may also be bought from bird and Audubon stores along with special wild bird seed mixes. Suet may be hung from trees in close-meshed wire nets so that the squirrels cannot get at it easily.

Buying seeds for birds can become expensive. One way to reduce this expense is to grow many wild seeds in your own garden; another

Figure 4–3. Feeding stick is good for small birds.

way is to buy your seeds in bulk from farm grain stores, getting neighbors and other friends to go in together on the purchase so you can get quantities at much less cost per pound.

Hummingbirds take a special food, simply a solution of nine parts water to one part granulated sugar. Don't use honey instead of sugar as it causes a fungus to grow in the birds' beaks. A stronger sugar solution keeps hummers from looking for nectar, which they need also, and insects, which provide needed protein. So never make the mix stronger than 1:9 sugar to water.

Squirrels may become a hazard in your garden, stealing bird food and chasing the birds away. This can be avoided by putting the feeders on top of tall poles and covering the poles with about two feet of slick metal which squirrels cannot climb. (Used aluminum sheets can be bought from offset printers at low cost to use for this purpose.)

ADVENTURES IN FEEDING BIRDS

Every species and even every individual bird has a different character, different habits, and different quirks. By watching birds, both with and without binoculars, you can observe how they act, take pictures, and also write down notes in a looseleaf notebook about their more interesting actions. Some birds are very quarrelsome and cause other birds lots of trouble. Starlings may be this way. What can you do to prevent this? As stated earlier, putting springs on your bird feeder can prevent English sparrows from being too bothersome to other small birds. Narrow doors keep out large bullies. I once stopped such a bird bully when I was a boy by hitting him a few times lightly with a peashooter when he tried to annoy other birds. I think he actually came to realize he was being punished. Think of other things you might do, but *never do something that really hurts any bird.*

Other adventures happen when a hawk such as a sparrow, Sharp-shinned, or Cooper's hawk, attacks birds in your garden. How do the birds give warning and how do they escape these enemies? Each kind of bird may try a different way. Most dive for bushes or under eaves. Watch carefully and write down all you see. This way you become more and more knowledgeable about birds and their habits. Possibly you can try different ways to protect your birds from those that hunt them; but remember, this is part of the natural life and adventure of birds. A pile of brush is one such protection. You will surely see birds dive into this pile if they are near it when a hawk approaches.

What do your birds do when an owl comes around? Sometimes different kinds of birds mob an owl in the daytime. When such mobbing happens, take careful notes on how each bird acts. This is one of the great adventures in their lives and exciting for you to see. Birds act in different ways about owls. Which are the most successful in driving them away? My experience is that either crows or jays make the most noise until the owl leaves in disgust.

There are always character shows likely to be going on in your garden, especially if you have attracted many birds. Kingbirds may rise up from your trees and chase away hawks or crows, dive-bombing them very accurately. Hummingbirds are the most amazing aggressors of all, sometimes attacking even the largest hawk or a human being that comes too near their nests. Imagine this tiny David, scarcely an ounce in weight, attacking you, a hundred- to two-hundred-pound Goliath. Hummingbirds also pull all kinds of comical tricks when they chase other birds and act so funny about it, as if patting themselves on the back. But sometimes they come to grief as when they dash into mirrors or windows, or are attacked by large spiders or mantids. Watch, watch, watch, WATCH! There is no end to the interesting sights!

BIRD SHELTERS AND BIRD HOUSES

A roosting box (Figure 4–4) is one of the best of all shelters for small birds. Be sure to put the small hole for letting them in at the bottom; you might make two holes so two birds can come in or out at once. Small roosting places out of the snow or cold winds or sleet will save many lives, especially because a roost for several birds permits several warm bodies to help each other keep the warmth up inside the house. Of course a larger roosting box can be made for larger birds, though they withstand the cold much better than the small birds because of their larger bodies and more and deeper feathers. Natural bird shelters such as fir and redwood trees have overlapping, tight needles which shed rain or snow, and many birds find fine shelters from storms in the hearts of such trees. Regular bird houses left up for the winter also will shelter many birds from storm.

Many bird houses and how to build them are illustrated in Figure 4–5. Be sure that each house has no rough edges or nails sticking out and that it is cleaned at least once a year, wiping the nest with mineral oil to get rid of mites and other pests that bother or even kill birds. Almost all bird houses should have hinged tops or sides so you can look in occasionally and see what is happening, trying to do so when the parents are gone because if you disturb one on a nest it may not come back. It is also possible to put a hinged door on the side of the house and place a clear plastic sheet over the side inside the door so you can look in on the occupants once in awhile, especially when the young birds are active, to see what they are doing and how they are getting along (Figure 4–6). At night you will disturb the birds least by opening the hinged door very quietly and gently and watching them through the plastic with a red-plastic-covered flashlight that gives out

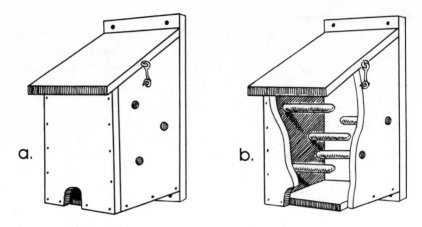

Figure 4–4. Roosting box. (*a*) Outside view. (*b*) Cutaway view.

only red light. The birds are disturbed very little by this red light and will act perfectly natural. Be careful not to drive out the bird at night, as it could freeze or be caught by an owl.

Cleaning out nest boxes is best done in late winter, around mid-February in the southern states and most of California and in mid-March or later in the northern states. This cleaning is important because of the blow fly, an insect that parasitizes and kills many birds. It attacks the young birds soon after they come out of the eggs and burrows inside them as parasites. The main way to stop this fly from its dirty work is to clean out the nests when the spring's first warmth begins, leaving the trash from the nest on the ground without burning it. In this trash there are usually some eggs or grubs of the chalcid fly which is an enemy of the blow fly. It parasitizes the blow fly and kills it before it can do harm to the young birds. If you clean out the nest boxes too soon, or destroy the trash from the nest, you will expose the chalcid flies to either the cold or fire and they will not be left alive to fight the birds' worst enemy, the blow fly.

Sizes of typical bird nest boxes are given in the following table:

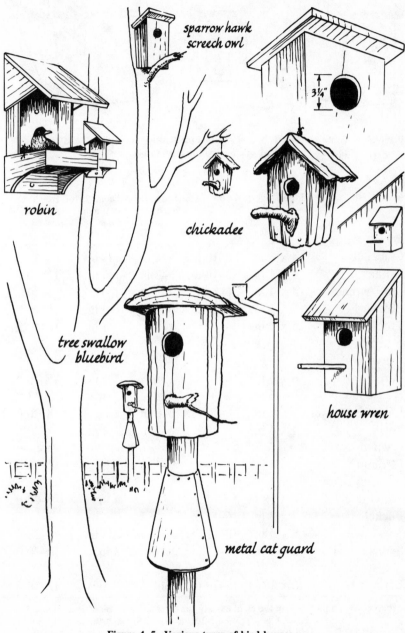

sparrow hawk
screech owl

3¼"

robin

chickadee

tree swallow
bluebird

house wren

metal cat guard

Figure 4–5. Various types of bird houses.

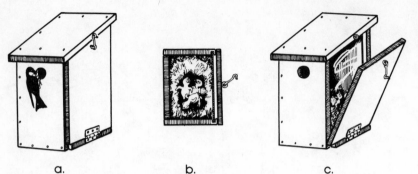

a.   b.   c.

Figure 4–6. Nesting box with hinged side and plastic "window." (a) Closed box. (b) Cutaway view from top. (c) Hinged side opened for observation.

Name	Floor	Depth	Above floor height of entrance	Diameter of entrance hole	Height to place above ground
Chickadee	4 x 4 in.	8–10 in.	6–8 in.	1⅛ in.	6–15 ft.
Nuthatch	4 x 4 in.	8–10 in.	6–8 in.	1¼ in.	12–20 ft
Most wrens	4 x 4 in.	6–8 in.	4–6 in.	1–1½ in.	6–10 ft.
Bluebird	5 x 5 in.	8 in.	6 in.	1½ in.	5–10 ft.
Tree & vegetable swallow	5 x 5 in.	6 in.	1–5 in.	1½ in.	10–15 ft.
Purple martin*	6 x 6 in.	6 in.	1 in.	2½ in.	15–20 ft.
House finch	6 x 6 in.	6 in.	4 in.	2 in.	8–13 ft.
Large flycatcher	6 x 6 in.	8–10 in.	6–8 in.	2 in.	8–20 ft.
Small woodpecker	4 x 4 in.	8–10 in.	6–8 in.	1¼ in.	7–20 ft.
Medium woodpecker	6 x 6 in.	12–16 in.	9–12 in.	2 in.	12–20 ft.
Wood duck	10 x 18 in.	10–24 in.	12–16 in.	4 in.	10–20 ft
Flicker	7 x 7 in.	16–19 in.	14–16 in.	2½ in.	7–20 ft.
Small owl	6 x 6 in.	10–12 in.	8–10 in.	2½ in.	10–20 ft.
Screech owl or sparrow hawk	8 x 8 in.	12–15 in.	9–12 in.	3 in.	10–30 ft.
Barn owl	10 x 18 in.	15–20 in.	4 in.	6 in.	12–20 ft.

*This is one compartment of the eight usually put together for a colony (see Figure 4–10).
Source: *Houses for Birds*, Conservation Bulletin 14, U. S. Department of the Interior, Washington, D.C. Sold by Superintendent of Documents, U. S. Government Printing Office, Washington, D.C. 20025.

Be sure to make your different houses fit the kinds of birds you want to attract. Figure 4–5 shows a number of different bird houses, as well as how to make a metal cat or squirrel guard. Figure 4–7 shows another simple design that would suit most birds, but remember that sizes, especially of the holes and other features, need to fit the different birds.

How to put up a nesting box in a tree or on a post is illustrated in Figure 4–8. Never put up a house with the hole pointing toward the sky, as too much rain can come in, and always try to orient the bird house facing away from the prevailing wind. A box should generally slope slightly downward, and you should put holes in the bottom so that any liquid will drain out of it. The top or side should be hinged for easy examination and cleaning.

Figure 4–6 shows how to build a bird house for observing the birds inside by using a plastic sheet fitted in a groove that is removable when you clean the nest box and protects the birds when the side door is opened. As noted earlier, you can observe the birds at night without disturbing them by using a red-covered flashlight that emits red light only.

A beautiful tree swallow nest box and plans for making it are shown in Figure 4–9. It is called the Kinney Tree Swallow Nest Box and is

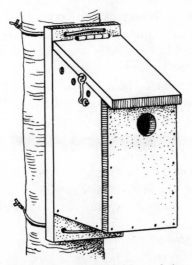

Figure 4–7. A simple bird house design.

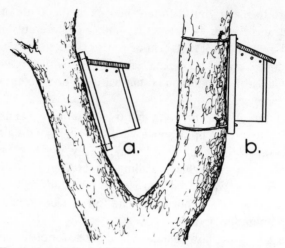

Figure 4–8. Hanging a bird house. (*a*) **Wrong way—tilted upward so that rain comes in door hole, and with nails, which may allow infection to enter tree.** (*b*) **Right way—level or tilted slightly downward so that rain does not enter, and with wires, which do not harm tree.**

adapted from the *Bulletin of the Massachusetts Audubon Society* (March, 1952). This nest is placed on top of a 2- to 3-inch- diameter post that puts the birds at least ten feet off the ground. The post needs a metal sheet, such as an aluminum plate obtained from an offset printing shop, to be placed around it to keep cats and other predators from climbing up. Plyboard, at least ⅜ inch thick, can be used for the different parts of the nest. The bird box should be at least ten inches long and seven inches wide, with the backboard at least six inches high and the front-board about 8 or 9 inches. The backboard is hinged and has a hook so it can be opened to look inside and see how the babies are doing or for later cleaning of the nest. The main entrance hole for the adult birds is 1¾ inches wide. Three other 1-inch holes can be cut for the baby birds to put out their heads for food. The T-shaped perch is a gift to the male so he can stand guard on it over the nest when not gathering food for the young. This is especially good for him when the female is incubating the eggs. Paint the whole house with waterproof paint when finished.

Figure 4–10 shows the grand apartment house of the purple martins, with rooms for eighteen families in a colony. New sets of nine

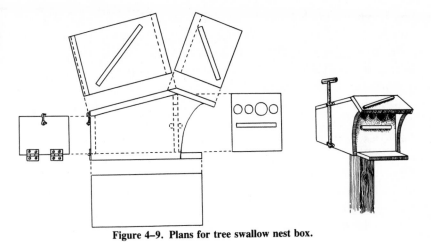

Figure 4–9. Plans for tree swallow nest box.

rooms can be added and all are held together by hooks and screw eyes so that the sections can be taken apart for early cleaning in the spring, and so new sets of nine apartments can be added if the martin colony grows.

Three-eighths-inch plyboard is used for most of the house construction. Since each apartment must be at least 6 by 6 inches in size, the main part of the building is 20½ by 20½ inches, but the plyboard to which each section is nailed must be 26 by 26 inches, allowing a 2¼-inch platform all around the outside. The base board of the lower

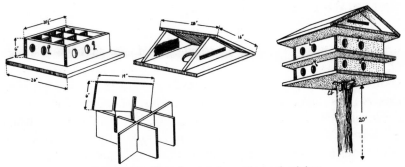

Figure 4–10. Plans for purple martin condominium.

apartment section is then placed on top of another 3/8-inch or 1/2-inch board, 26 by 26 inches, that is centered above and nailed quite firmly to the top of the post. The lower section of nine apartments is attached to this by either screws or bolts so it can be easily detached in winter for cleaning. The second apartment section fits above when it is needed and on top of this is a roof section 28 by 28 inches in size to give protection against too much rain blowing into the nest holes. Holes in the sides of the apartments should be 2½ inches in size to keep out larger predators. The supporting pole should be six inches square, at least ten feet high, and of good hardwood for strength. It should be put firmly into the ground eighteen inches or more with cement all around it, and extra strength added by 2 by 4s nailed against either side at the base. Holes in the eaves allow air to flow under the roof for good ventilation.

This martin colony apartment house gives tremendous opportunities for watching bird behavior in a colony at close hand; the different birds are found to have different personalities and can be watched closely for both humorous and critical incidents. What dangers do they face and how do they face them? Hawks like the Cooper's, who attack birds by diving at them from trees, are probably the most dangerous.

Plastic cartons or tin cans can be used to make very quickly put-together bird houses which can be nailed or glued to boards and put up on posts wherever desired (Figure 4–11). For dimensions, refer to the chart given earlier of sizes of bird nest boxes. Such carton houses probably should be replaced with new ones each year, as they are not very durable.

MATERIALS FOR BIRD NESTS

A basket or box of materials that birds can use in making their nests can be placed out for them to find. But do not put out any strings or ropes longer than twelve inches because birds can get wrapped or knotted in long strings of any kind and strangle to death. Hair cuttings, short strings, bits of old ropes, wool cuttings, bits of clothing or other cloth, ribbons, straw, old hay (as long as it is not moldy), and many other such things can be put out for the birds to help with their nests. Sometimes birds use peculiar things for their nests; for example, swallows have been seen happily gathering chicken feathers.

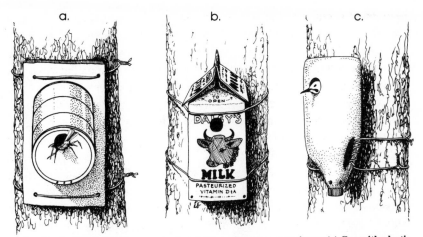

Figure 4–11. Simple bird houses constructed from common containers. (*a*) Can with plastic lid mounted on board and wired to tree with holes in bottom to allow moisture to drain. (*b*) Milk carton with wider flap stapled to top to keep out rain. (*c*) Well-rinsed bleach bottle with holes in bottom to allow moisture to drain out.

OBSERVING BIRD BEHAVIOR

After you get all kinds of birds happily coming to your back yard and gardens, what then? The fact is you probably have by that time the equivalent of a three- or four-ring circus going on in your yard and gardens—and for all the year, if you help birds stay alive through the winter with the proper food and shelter. But it is a circus that never gets boring for new birds always are likely to appear and bring you new thrills and experiences. Here are just a few suggestions for increasing the variety of your experiences with birds and getting to know them better. Use these suggestions to stimulate other ideas of your own.

One thing that will help you see interesting happenings you might miss otherwise is to rig up ways to observe your birds without their realizing they are being observed. One way is to fix up a disguised watching place or blind in your yard, such as those already illustrated in Figure 3–5. Have a comfortable chair and pillow in your blind so you can sit still without getting fidgety, and have binoculars handy to see close-up what is happening at the food and water stations and the bird houses. If you have several kinds of birds present, you should not have long to wait, and at the very least you can hear and watch birds singing and calling, and learn to identify them by both their appearance and their sounds.

There is great rivalry between some bird species, as between the starlings and the flickers over feeding and nesting places, and between the owls and most other birds if ever an owl is caught in the open. Also, hummingbirds and kingbirds like to lord it over other birds, and the rivalry between different or the same species of hummers may be both tremendous and very funny.

How birds catch insects and how insects defend themselves from birds are constant sources of new chances to understand behavior. If you have any large mantises in your garden, you may see how they outbluff the birds and even sometimes catch and kill a smaller one. Large dragonflies have been known to attack hummingbirds. Watch for this!

What do moths do about their bird and bat enemies? Some moths have been known to exhibit fantastic evasive techniques to avoid bats and birds. Watch for this in the evening, using a flashlight or other bright light if possible. Write observations in your notes.

If you have a bird feeder on your windowsill, you may want to put a lace curtain between you and the birds so you can watch them close at hand but not be seen. You will see how some birds are bullies and drive other birds away from the food. I have already discussed ways you can stop this. Still another way of watching birds without being seen is to rig up a long tube, or periscope, with a mirror inside (Figure 4–12), so you can watch birds around a corner of your house without being seen. This can also be used like a periscope to look over hedges and see what is happening on the other side or even placed inside a hedge where you can watch birds and their young in a nest without disturbing them. Since mirrors work both ways, put a dark cloth over your end and put your head under it while observing birds.

SCIENTIFIC PROJECTS WITH BIRDS

There are some simple scientific projects you can do with birds that will help increase your knowledge and train you in close observation, a valuable thing for anybody to learn. Here are just a few. You can visit the nearest college biology department or museum and ask for other suggestions about things you can do.

Figure 4–12. Periscope for observing birds. Unless the viewer holds periscope tightly to face to block out light, the subject can look into the periscope and see the viewer.

1. If you can get an owl(s) to nest in one of your bird boxes or even find one that is nesting under the eaves of your house or in a hollow tree, you can study its food habits by examining daily the pellets of hair and bones that owls drop from their perches at night after they have digested a meal. These dry little pellets can be taken apart with tweezers and all their contents, particularly the bones and skulls of prey animals, can be spread out on a large clean white paper and analyzed. The skulls can be identified as to the species of mice, rats, or rabbits they come from (refer to a field guide or ask a biologist for help). Then you can set about counting the exact number of kinds of animals the owls devour over a period of weeks, months, or even years. Your records of this, if properly done, will be valuable to scientists and science.

2. Study the percentage of birds of certain species who use their bills or feet for finding food and the different ways they do this.

3. Take one bird species and study all the ways it uses to escape enemies and, if possible, what percentage each way is used.

4. Chart your garden on a map to show bird territories, marking each territory and each species. Learn how territories are established and how they change under changing circumstances.

5

Special Methods for Observing Birds

THE BEHAVIOR OF birds is varied and fascinating. This chapter describes several ways of watching the activities of birds in different circumstances.

EXPERIMENTS WITH BIRD-FEEDING STATIONS

Bird-feeding stations can be rigged up to test the intelligence and agility of different birds and animals. For example, if you have tree squirrels in your garden or nearby trees that you can attract to a special bird-and-squirrel-feeding station, rig up steps that the squirrels can use to jump from one to another to reach the station and find food. Then gradually increase the distance between the steps day-by-day so the squirrels have to jump farther each day. In this way you can determine the length of their greatest leap. By rigging one of the steps to a spring wire that causes it to drop or rise when the squirrel lands on this step, you can observe his reaction and how he overcomes his difficulty. You also can surround the feeding station with walls, but with a special sliding door that can be slid aside to open, and see if the squirrel(s) can learn to slide this door open to get at the food.

To study the learning ability of birds, you can hang a bird-feeding station from a line so you can drop it a few inches if one bird on the station attacks or bullies another bird. See how long it takes for you to teach such a bird to act like a gentleman or lady, and leave the other birds alone. Another interesting activity is to tape the voices of the birds at the feeder and then play back the different voices at other times when the birds feed to see how they respond to the sounds. You also can set up a cloth on a frame over the feeder so that you can suddenly drop the cloth down and cover the feeder while the birds are on it. See which birds are too fast or too clever to be caught this way and which learn after a while not to be afraid of the cloth since it will not hurt them at all.

A comfort-feeding station with maze can be built to study the reactions of birds and squirrels to heat during cold weather. This device is completely weatherproof and has an electric line connected to an electric heating pad. Such a warm feeding station provides comfort to birds and squirrels on cold days, particularly in winter, and can be used to observe how they react with each other about the heat. The heated area can also be placed at the end of a maze and have food with it so as to be a double attraction to the creatures to figure out the maze and reach the area of heat and food. Be sure that your electric line is well insulated so that water cannot get to it and short it. Only turn on the line when you can watch it so that no accidents will happen. Probably only low heat would be used most of the time on the electric pad; but if you watch closely and do not use the heat to be cruel to the animals, you can turn up the heat gradually to see what their reaction is as it gets warmer.

INTERACTION OF STUFFED OWL WITH BIRDS IN TREES

Owls that get caught out in a tree in the daylight are often badgered or attacked by other birds, particularly jays, kingbirds, chickadees, crows, magpies, and sparrows. If you can obtain, make, or copy a stuffed owl (Figure 5–2), perhaps even using a lifelike toy owl of the right size (that is, eight to ten inches for a screech owl, or seven to eight inches for a Saw-whet owl), you can rig this as a movable dummy in a tree and watch through binoculars from a comfortable distance how the birds react to it.

The owl must be rigged with almost invisible fish line or threads that you can manipulate from your distance so it moves. If done cleverly enough, you can actually make the owl raise its wings as if attacking a bird. This realistic attack on the part of the owl will greatly excite the other birds and cause them to ring the owl even closer or to move back in fear. What they do will give you a fine example of the behavior of the birds who are bothering it. Some of what happens will likely be quite comical, and you can have a good laugh about the matter if you do not laugh too loud.

Another way to do this and be even closer to the activities is to build a blind as described previously (Figure 3–5), and place this blind near the owl tree while making sure the eye slot in the blind allows you to see the "owl" clearly where you have it perched. To see the owl at night and other owls that are attracted to it, it would be necessary to have a powerful flashlight covered with red plastic so that it sends a red beam towards the dummy owl. This red beam will probably not disturb the other owls because they are not sensitive usually to red light.

How a real owl reacts to your fake one is also interesting to see. However, if the real owl is a great horned owl, you had better get your "owl" down out of the tree quickly as this large owl is likely to attack and destroy the dummy. If the real owl is a small one, it will probably call at first to your "owl," then begin to creep or flit closer and closer until it finds your "owl" is a fake. If you can mimic owl sounds with your voice, you can make the situation rather confusing and observe how the real owl reacts to both a fake owl and owl sounds.

CONVERSING WITH CROWS

Crows usually rest in some woods for the night. Watch carefully to find out where their night-sleeping location is, then go there by daylight when they are gone and build a brush-covered or other kind of blind (Figure 3–5). Hide in this blind before the crows come at nightfall and have a small portable tape recorder with magnifying disc to record their evening calls as they talk together (also record their morning calls if you can). Go back another evening, before the birds arrive, with the tape recorder and a loud speaker. Do not play all the

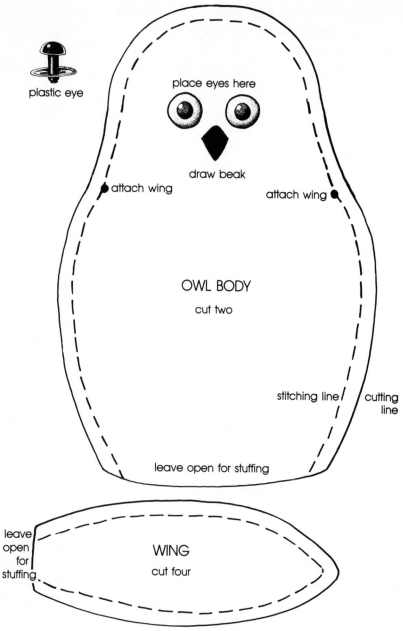

plastic eye

place eyes here

draw beak

attach wing

attach wing

OWL BODY

cut two

stitching line

cutting line

leave open for stuffing

leave open for stuffing

WING

cut four

Figure 5–1. Dummy owl pattern.

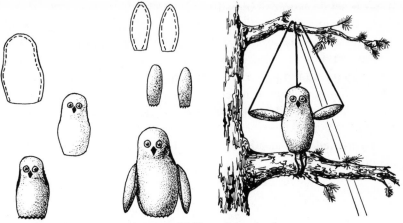

Figure 5–2. Making a dummy owl.

Note: All seams ¼ inch.

Owl body:
1. Cut two owl body pieces from brown fabric.
2. Sew pieces right sides together, leaving bottom open for stuffing.
3. Turn owl body right side out.
4. Draw beak on face where indicated.
5. Attach eyes on front where indicated.
6. Fill firmly with polyester stuffing. Whip stitch bottom closed.

Owl wings:
1. Cut four wing pieces from brown fabric.
2. For each wing, sew pieces right sides together leaving base open for stuffing.
3. Turn right side out.
4. Fill with polyester stuffing. Whip stitch base closed.

Assembling owl:
1. Whip stitch wings to body.
2. Attach fishing line to top of head and tips of wings.
3. Locate suitable tree where there is a wide variety of perching birds present for you to observe.
4. Run wire through bottom of owl body and around a limb to secure.
5. Support upright by tying fishing line from top of head to a branch located directly above model.
6. Run fishing line from wings over upper branch to hiding place or blind. Pull wing lines to make owl flap wings.

taped crow calls at once from the blind, but play separate calls to the crows at intervals. Carefully note their reactions to the different calls. In this way you can learn something about crow language, while at the same time have an amusing conversation with them through the use of the tape. They will probably be quite astonished at what they hear.

If, by practice, you can imitate some of these calls yourself, you can have even more fun with them. Write all of this down in your notebook.

You may also learn many other things about crows' habits. Write them down! For example, crows sometimes seem to punish one of their members for an infraction of a rule. They seem to actually sit in judgment deciding what punishment to give the criminal. I have even seen such a crow executed by three other crows! He was punished for poorly guarding against the attack of a hawk. In another instance, a crow was apparently telling of an adventure it had, for all its friends were listening intently.

ADVENTURES WITH REPTILES

6

Snakes

IT IS A great shame that so many people are afraid of or don't like snakes. Not only are they great allies of mankind, for the most part, but many kinds can be befriended very easily, and some make excellent pets. The fear of snakes is almost entirely due to emotional conditioning since all snakes in North America except the comparatively uncommon poisonous ones are incapable of doing serious harm to humans. Some snakes, like the garter snakes, are unpleasant to handle because they give off offensive-smelling secretions. The poisonous snakes (Figure 6–1) actually do good in the wild by keeping down the numbers of rats, mice, rabbits, and similar creatures who, if they became too numerous, would seriously damage the food supplies of mankind. Also, most poisonous snakes in North America, with the exception of the very large diamond-backed rattlesnakes or the water moccasin occasionally, rarely attack people, but almost universally try to get away by taking cover in brush or water.

Studying snakes' habits and behavior and how they interact with other living things usually requires sitting still and watching for long

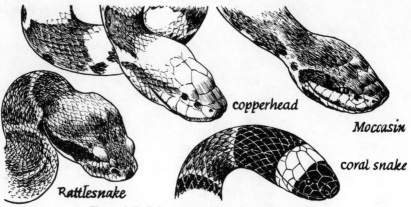

Figure 6–1. Poisonous snakes in the United States.

periods, or moving very slowly and cautiously, or placing baits to entice them to come near, or capturing them to put in cages or terrariums.

CATCHING SNAKES

A fishing or other pole with the line formed into a loop with a bowline knot at the end can be used to capture snakes by dropping the noose over the head and drawing it tight as shown in Figure 7–2. The snake, which must not be a poisonous snake, can then be dropped into a jar with a lid if it's small, or into a sack with a drawstring if it's large. The lid on the jar must have holes to give air to the reptile. You can also pin a snake down with a long stick and then grasp it firmly just behind the head so it cannot bite. Some large nonpoisonous snakes, like gopher snakes or racers, can give a somewhat painful but rarely dangerous bite. *Leave poisonous snakes totally alone unless you have been trained by an expert to handle them.*

KEEPING SNAKES IN CAPTIVITY

Since the whole effort of most snakes when they know they have been seen by a human is to get away into brush, water, or a hole where they can hide, you either have to find them when they are off-guard and immediately freeze so as not to scare them, or try to capture one and watch it in captivity. Cages (Figure 6–2) and terrariums (Figure 7–3) should always be big enough to give the snake placed in them plenty of room. You should fix rocks and plants about to create the habitat that is familiar to the snake. If you keep snakes in cages or other enclosures you have to make sure that they have enough water and food and are not exposed to either too much heat or too much cold. When I keep snakes in cages for the winter, I always have a light bulb going inside the cage to provide a modicum of heat even when the cage is inside the house.

I strongly advise that you not keep snakes or other animals in captivity any more than a few days for observation. Always release them into the habitat they came from or something very close to it. If you keep large snakes very long, you normally need to raise mice, rats, or rabbits to supply them with food. It is interesting, of course, to watch how one of these animals is captured and killed by the snake. A gopher, rat, or king snake usually kills by constriction, which makes the prey easier to swallow; but, a racer or water snake generally kills by a bite and then swallows the whole animal. White mice often can be obtained from a pet store, and wild mice can be captured from nests

shows habitat   *shows back door and sand tray*

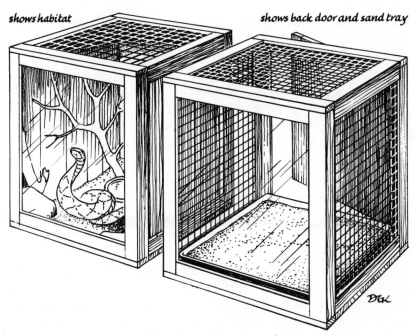

Figure 6–2. Cages for keeping snakes.

in an old barn. A barrel with food in the bottom and a ramp leading to it often acts as a trap for mice. Catch them also in a jar, clapping on a cover quickly.

BEHAVIOR OF DIFFERENT SNAKES

Each kind of snake usually has a different way of frightening or escaping from enemies. Some interesting snakes are shown in Figure 6–3.

The rattlesnake usually buzzes its rattle to scare you away. It is certainly wise to keep clear of this dangerous creature whose poison can make you very sick or even kill you. When a rattlesnake knows it cannot escape by moving into a hole or pile of rocks or thick brush, it stands its ground bravely by coiling and preparing to strike. In the wild, I leave rattlesnakes alone as they are a part of the balance of life. I will kill one with a stick or shovel if it is near a home, as it is dangerous to children. Do not be cruel by teasing a snake or striking merely to hurt. Strike to kill by smashing the head and stay far away. The rattles, by the way, do not tell how old the snake is. Rattles are lost by being torn off in brush, and a snake may also grow more than one rattle each year.

Gopher or bull snakes play a game with you by rattling their tails in dry leaves, making the ignorant person think they are a rattlesnake, but you can always tell them apart by the head and neck. In a gopher snake and most common snakes, the head and neck are almost the same width, while in a rattlesnake the head is much wider than the neck. Gopher snakes do a lot of their hunting underground in the holes of gophers and mice.

Racers and whipsnakes zip along at high speed through the grass or brush and may even climb a bush or a tree. They generally are not easy to handle without being bitten. If you are quiet and they do not see you, perhaps you can see them steal an egg from a bird's nest in a bush, one of their favorite ways of getting food.

The hog-nosed snake, found in most places except the Far West, is remarkable by being so amusing. If molested, it hisses, spreads its head, and strikes ferociously as if it were poisonous, but actually it never bites. If you still attack, it rolls over and plays dead. As a final indignity it may make a loud plopping noise from its rear end. Actually,

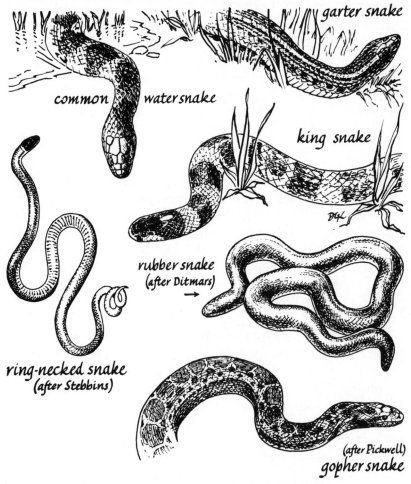

Figure 6–3. Some nonpoisonous snakes in the United States.

this is one of the easiest of all snakes to tame and is good to keep in captivity as long as you give it plenty of water and toads.

The little ring-necked snake has a yellow-to-orange ring behind the head and may coil its reddish-orange tail up into a corkscrew to try to scare you into thinking it can sting. Ring-necked snakes are easily tamed and feed on insects and worms.

Water snakes are rather stout-bodied and are found mainly in the East, while garter snakes are narrower and are found everywhere, some being just as water-loving as the water snakes. All are rather strong fighters if handled, but the garter snakes usually also give off an offensively smelling fluid to force you to leave them alone. It is fascinating to see these snakes wiggling at high speed through the water and even diving down to deeper depths to get away from you.

King snakes are about the most beautiful of all snakes, especially the mountain king snake and the milk snake, which copy the poisonous coral snake by having black, red, and yellow rings, but with the red touched on both sides by black whereas the coral snake has the red with both sides touched by yellow. This makes the king snake look dangerous to most creatures and so they are left alone. (Remember: red and yellow kill a fellow; red and black, poison lack!) I once saw a California mountain king snake that had just changed its skin so that the red, black, and yellow bands literally glistened and sparkled—they were stunningly beautiful. King snakes kill rattlesnakes and lizards by their powerful constriction ability and may be immune to the poison.

SUGGESTED PROJECTS WITH SNAKES

1. The racetrack used to test the speed of lizards (Figure 7–4) can be used also to test the speed of snakes. However, do not be tempted to tease the snake into moving fast; by walking around the outside of the ring you may cause the snake to move rapidly. You can also put a prey animal such as a lizard or insect in with the snake and see if it will chase the prey. Use a stopwatch to time the snake's movement, and record the speeds in your notebook or journal. The racers and whipsnakes will probably be, by far, the fastest snakes you will encounter, although garter snakes are quite fast, too. Remember to let all snakes go when there is no need to watch them anymore.

2. Determine which temperatures make the snake most active and which slow it up the most. But do not force any snake to stay in very hot or very cold temperatures as these can kill them. Keep records of their activities and the temperatures that go with them in your notebook. Tempt a snake with live food such as a frog, small lizard, or insect and see what temperatures cause the most activity when these creatures are seen.

3. Keep several snakes of the same species in a large terrarium together, well fed, and watered and see how they interact with each other. Is there any courting and mating? Any antagonism or forming

of territories? Any signs of other kinds of communication between the snakes? If you keep a record of temperatures and humidity, you can see how these effect the actions of your snakes. Keep notes on all you see. Sometimes snakes coil about each other and seem to enjoy the contact.

4. Snakes change their skins in order to grow bigger. The old skin may become very rough-looking and dull so you know when a snake is about to shed. Some snakes have a rather hard time getting rid of the old skin, especially around the eyes, which makes some of them very short-tempered at that time. How do they get rid of difficult skin patches? Usually by rubbing on something rough. Watch and see!

Many other similar projects can be done with snakes if you watch and get to know them. But always be kind! They are really our friends!

7

Lizards

LIZARDS ARE EXTREMELY interesting creatures and almost completely harmless except for the gila monster in the Arizona and southern Nevada desert country. Even the gila monster is shy and tries to get away from you, and would not bite unless you actually stepped on one or grabbed it. But it is ridiculous for people to be afraid of other lizards. They are not even slimy, as some people believe, but have dry, scaly skin, which is good protection against enemies and the drying effect of the sun. There is one smooth-skinned lizard in the deserts, the gecko, and the green anole of the southern states (sometimes called a "chameleon") is comparatively smooth-skinned. The male anole has a flap of skin on its throat which it may suddenly flare out like a bright red flag to attract a mate or scare off another male. This, like the blue bellies that fence lizards display by bobbing their bodies, is not a sign of any danger to man, as some foolish people believe.

Several different lizards are shown in Figure 7–1. Many kinds can be easily tamed and become quite good pets. Geckos or anoles are especially good to have around your house where they climb up and down the walls and even on the ceiling. They catch flies and cockroaches and are good at removing other pests. I once had an anole as a pet that loved to climb up and perch on my shoulder or put its head against my throat.

CATCHING LIZARDS

You can capture some lizards by simply moving up very slowly and suddenly shooting out your hand to grab them. Horned lizards (wrongly called horned toads), can be caught this way, as can fence lizards sometimes. Others, like the racerunners and the leopard or collared lizards, are far too fast and shy in most cases. These can be caught with a long fishing pole with a bowline slip-knot (Figure 7–2) on the end. Even with this, however, you have to move very slowly and cautiously until you can slip the noose over the head and draw it tight about the neck. Do not continue to choke the lizard once caught, but immediately catch the lizard firmly in your hand, holding it by the neck so it cannot bite (the bite is usually comparatively harmless) and slipping it into a cloth bag with a drawstring for closing it at the top. Do not mix two different species in the same bag because one may kill and eat the other.

One trick I use for approaching these lizards is to stand perfectly still while they are looking in my direction, but move slowly towards them while they are looking in the opposite direction, then freeze when they turn their heads. Careful stalking reaps the best rewards!

LIZARDS IN CAPTIVITY

Lizards are best kept in well-made and clean terrariums generally larger than those needed for insects alone. Refer to books in the References for information on the kind of food each is accustomed to eating. Keep them well fed and watered at all times, letting them go as soon as you no longer have need for them. Figure 7–3 shows examples of terrariums. Be sure your terrarium has the kind of habitat in it that is natural to any particular lizard.

Most lizards feed on insects or worms though some of the larger ones catch and kill other lizards or even small snakes and mammals. Some, like the chuckwalla, feed on plants. How they capture insects can be seen when you let loose such insects into their terrariums. It is usually done by careful stalking. A continuous supply of insect larvae

GILA MONSTER

RACERUNNER

CHUCKWALLA

GECKO

ANOLE

WESTERN FENCE
LIZARD

COLLARED LIZARD

HORNED LIZARD

LEOPARD LIZARD

Figure 7–1 Some lizards found in the United States.

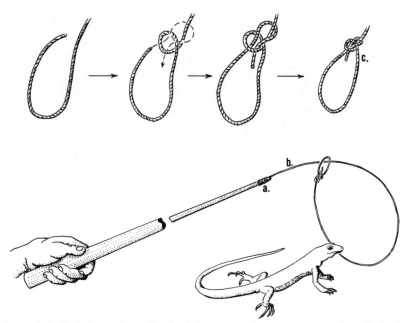

Figure 7–2. Tool for snaring a lizard. (*a*) Secure thread or fishing line to the end of a 6-to 8-foot-long pole. (*b*) Shank of thread should be no more than 6 inches long with noose open. Make loop for noose by tying a bowline knot (*c*) at end of thread and pulling shank through. Use No. 50 thread for small lizards; No. 8 thread, fishline, or leader for larger lizards.

to feed to lizards in captivity can be obtained from a pet shop where they use the yellow meal worms of the darkling beetle, *Tenebrio molitor,* as food for birds, etc. These worms and their adults multiply wherever grain is stored and they can get at it. By raising your own meal worms on spoiled grain, obtainable at farms or in a box of cornmeal, you can keep your lizards happy.

Use other insects for experiments on how lizards catch them and how the insects may escape. A large preying mantis may give a small lizard a good fight for its money, though usually lizards pounce and catch insects almost instantly in their well-armored mouths. It is too bad lizards don't hunt only insects that are harmful to man rather than taking most any insects they see. Sometimes they get a surprise in finding a bad-tasting insect such as a monarch butterfly caterpiller, or an insect like a bombardier beetle that shoots poison gas at them, or are stung by a dangerous big wasp like the pepsis wasp that captures

Figure 7–3. Simple cages for reptiles and amphibians with habitat background.

and paralyzes tarantulas. How insects handle such situations is always intriguing and sometimes quite comical to see. Keep your eyes open and your notes written in your notebook.

EXPERIMENTS WITH LIZARDS

1. Chuckwallas (Fig. 7–1), who live in rocky deserts of the Southwest, escape from enemies by crawling quickly into crevices between rocks and inflating themselves with air so they are wedged tightly in place. If you are in good chuckwalla country, you can spend an exciting day seeing how many chuckwallas you can find that use this trick and if any of the enemies of chuckwallas, such as the white-tailed kite, the prairie falcon, or the leopard lizard, can overcome such tricks and catch a chuckwalla. If you want a chuckwalla for a pet, use a wire to gradually and gently force it out of its crevice.

2. Geckos of the Southwest and the green anole lizard (sometimes called a chameleon) of the southern states both can climb upside down along ceilings and are also expert on sheer cliffs and other rocks. Watch

carefully how they do this and examine their padded or suction-cupped toes. Also see if you can dislodge them without hurting them, using a long slender stick, and watch what they do when they fall. Do they land on all four feet like a cat or do they fall more clumsily? Even if dislodged from a ceiling, these lizards cannot really be hurt because their small size and weight does not let them fall hard.

Because geckos and anoles are tremendous fly catchers and eaters, they do a lot of good for mankind. They also catch mosquitoes and other harmful creatures. Observe how they camouflage themselves, even changing colors, and how they cautiously approach a fly, then suddenly rush and seize it. Watch one for an hour or two and observe how many flies it catches and how many it loses. Then try others and discover if some are more accurate and successful than the rest and why this is so.

3. The courtship and mating of lizards is still only partly understood. How does an anole use the brilliant colors it displays in a kind of fan on its throat to attract a female or drive away other males? Is there ever any actual fighting or are the throat fan and its colors enough to frighten away rivals from one male anole's territory? Blue-bellied or fence lizards, collared lizards, and leopard lizards exhibit similar flashing of colors. Discover the differences between such lizards. Almost all male lizards bob up and down with their bodies when flashing colors, but do they do this differently in different species?

Very little is known about the courtship of some of the horned lizards, which are found mainly in the West. These are among the most comical of lizards in their actions, and yet they effectively use their horns to keep free of attackers. Examine their escapes from attack, their courtship, and their methods of feeding. They are also very good at camouflage.

4. Some lizards, like the collared lizard, work up to high speed and then suddenly start running on their hind legs alone. If you can catch such high-speed lizards with the fish pole and running noose method, then you can set up a race course to determine how fast they can run. Find a level piece of ground and place 2-to-4-foot-long boards one foot deep in a circle about a foot to a foot-and-a-half apart (Figure 7–4). Make a second circle inside the first one. You can, of course, make the circular racetrack as long as you have time, money, and patience to do so. Attach light plastic sheeting or aluminum plates,

bought from offset printing shops, to the stakes to form the sides of the racetrack.

Do not try to make the lizard run by hurting it. But you could run lightly around the track behind it so it thinks it is being chased. Have a friend with a stopwatch time the run from start to finish, which should be at the same point. If the lizard does not run that far, measure the distance it does run before stopping and time it for that distance. Do not run the lizard until it is exhausted.

See if you can determine the fastest racing times for several different lizards. Find out if the lizards that run on their hind legs can go faster than those that run on four. Do you notice that fast lizards do not need as much camouflage as those that are slow? Lizards like the geckos can actually change color to be camouflaged in different surroundings.

To catch a lizard in the racetrack, have a place in the track where you can slip two boards down through the slots and enclose the lizard between them. This has to be done very carefully and slowly so as not to disturb the lizard. Lizards should be let free unless you have some specific experiment to try with them. Always think of them as living

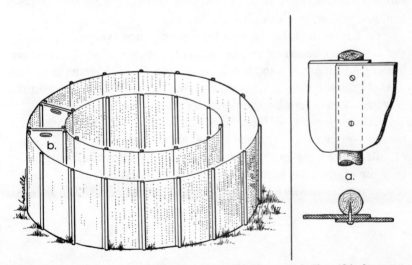

Figure 7–4. A lizard racetrack. Stakes are driven into the ground, 12 to 18 inches apart, to form two concentric circles. Aluminum printing plates are screwed to stakes as shown (*a*). Removable panels may be slid into brackets (*b*) in order to capture the lizard.

creatures needing respect and kindness; keep them well fed and watered, and let them go when no longer needed.

5. Horned lizards usually can be tamed easily and may make good pets. I had such a pet for several months. It loved to be petted and talked to. On a cold day, it liked the warmth of my hand or throat. See if you can train a horned lizard to come for food when called, jump over a low barrier, take a fly from your fingers, or respond when you sing or play music.

Study how a horned lizard reacts to heat. If you have one in a terrarium turn the terrarium so it is partially in the hot sun. What is the temperature where it is? See if it tries to get in the shade. Experiment with different temperatures and find which one or ones drive it to go to the shade, but do not force it to stay in the hot sunshine because it may die of heat stroke. At night, what temperature does it have to have to stay active? Does it ever bury itself in the sand of the terrarium to get away from the cold? What other interesting things does it do about cold and heat? How is it affected by humidity? Write down the answers to all these questions. They will help you learn much about these interesting little animals. You can study the courtship of horned lizards if you have one male and one female of the same species in the same terrarium. How is their courtship different from that of other lizards or other species of horned lizards?

6. To test how high a lizard can jump when escaping an enemy, put a barrier a couple of inches high in the middle of your lizard race-track. Run a lizard around the track and see if he can jump the barrier. Test with increasing heights adding one-half inch each time. In this way, you can determine the jumping ability of different species.

There are many different kinds of lizards and many other experiments you can do. Try finding how well a lizard can swim. Do any play dead like a possum? Which use camouflage most effectively? Keep thinking of many such questions and try them out on your lizards, but *always treat each with respect and kindness and let them go in a few days.*

8

Turtles and Tortoises

TURTLES AND TORTOISES (Figure 8–1) are vastly interesting creatures to observe and some make fine pets. However, you need to ask your local fish and wildlife people about which species you can catch and keep because some turtles and tortoises are protected from capture by law. If you do keep a turtle or tortoise for a pet, make sure it is well fed and watered daily or do not keep it at all. Turtles are sensitive and possibly intelligent creatures, and it is very sad to see one being mistreated or neglected. If you return a captive turtle to the wild, be sure to release it in a suitable habitat, preferably where you found it.

Watching turtles in the wild usually requires the greatest possible caution and care. If you are willing to sit beside a pond for hours without moving, you will in time likely see turtles come up out of the water onto a bank, island, or rock to bask themselves in the sun. Sometimes several turtles do this for company. In such cases you can see them scratch their ears or other parts of their bodies to get at the ticks, leeches, or other creatures that bother them, and you also see how quickly they slide down a bank and dive underwater if they feel that they are in danger. Some, like the sliders and the soft-shelled turtles

painted turtle

How to catch
a turtle
(see text)

spotted turtle →
(after Ditmars)

Western   pond turtle

pond terrapin
(after Ditmars)
→

box turtle–"turned"turtle
shows hinged plastron.
(after Ditmars)

desert tortoise (after Pickwell)

Figure 8–1. Some interesting turtles.

which look almost like flat pancakes, do this so rapidly the eye can
scarcely follow them.

If you have a snorkel and move extremely slowly underwater or
near the surface, watching all that is below you, and if the water is
fairly clear, you may be able to watch a turtle feeding underwater.
After you get back on land, write down all that you have seen. Most
turtles feed like cattle, browsing along on the underwater plants, but
almost all of them also will feed on insects, pollywogs, and other small
creatures if they can catch them. The turtle's usual method of catching
such prey is to hide among the plants until an insect or other creature

comes near and then to shoot out its long neck, snapping the insect with its jaws. But the soft-shelled turtles, or pancakes, are such fast swimmers and runners that they can catch many creatures by swimming or running them down.

The ugly-looking snapping turtle, which has a very large head and long tail, and the diamondback terrapins, with their knobby or spiny keels along the middle of the back, are more inclined to eat flesh than most other turtles. Both have powerful crushing jaws and it is very unwise to let them get hold of a hand or finger or foot. The snapping turtle often lies in the mud of a pond bottom, looking like part of the mud and, suddenly, shooting out its head and jaws to snap up a passing frog, insect, fish, or crayfish. The diamondback terrapins often live in brackish water or even salt marshes along the eastern and Gulf coasts where they eat a few plants, but mainly feed on clams and other mollusks, crayfish, crabs, shrimp, and other crustaceans they find on the plants or in the mud. They are much easier to watch when feeding than the snapping turtles.

CATCHING A TURTLE

All the water-loving turtles can be caught best by the buried barrel method. A barrel is wired tightly to a stake that has been driven into the bottom of a pond near the shore where turtles have been seen to gather (Figure 8–1). The top of the barrel must be sufficiently high out of the water so that a turtle cannot climb out. A flat board, wide enough for the turtle to walk on, is placed from the land out to the middle of the barrel and must be so balanced that when a turtle crawls out on the board to get the meat or other bait you put on the end of the board, its weight causes the board to tip and throw the turtle into the barrel. When catching a turtle in this way, never leave it in the barrel long enough to starve, but come around twice daily to see what you have captured.

KEEPING A TURTLE IN CAPTIVITY

Turtles may be kept in part-water terrariums that are big enough to give them plenty of room. Make the surroundings in the terrarium as much like a turtle's natural habitat as possible. Be sure it is fed regularly every day. What it feeds on are usually plants like lettuce and cabbage, insects, and small chunks of meat. You can learn about other things to feed it from books on turtles (and reptiles) listed in the References located at the end of this book. Many turtles make fine pets but some, like the diamondback terrapin and the snapping turtles and soft-shelled turtles, remain pugnacious for a long time and may give you a dangerous bite. Such turtles are safe to carry by the tail, provided you hold them away from your body and with their backs towards you.

LAND TURTLES

Tortoises, wood turtles, and box turtles often wander on land and generally are much easier to watch and have experiments with than the water-loving turtles. The tortoises are easily told by their stumpy legs (like an elephant's) and the lack of any webbing on their feet. The wood turtle is identified by its sculptured back, with a very rough shell that rises upward like an irregular pyramid in a series of concentric ridges and grooves. The box turtles are called by this name because they look like boxes when they close up their hinged "doors" or plastrons (the armor that covers their stomachs), both front and back. This gives them great protection when attacked by animals like a fox or wildcat. Box turtles make splendid pets in your backyard when fenced in, given a pan of water, a dry little house for shelter from the weather, and food such as berries, other fruits, raw hamburger, and table scraps. All these three kinds of turtles are found mainly in the East, except for the desert tortoise, which ranges through the southwestern deserts. Most of them dig holes in the ground where they sleep away the too hot or too cold days.

SOME PROJECTS WITH TORTOISES AND TURTLES

1. Follow a tortoise, a wood turtle, or a box turtle about for a day or two trying not to disturb it any more than necessary. Pace off the distances it covers between points like trees, large rocks, a road, etc. Draw a rough map of where it goes, marking on the map with numbers where it stopped to eat and putting in your notebook a description of what you saw it eat and how it did this or how it captured prey. This can be a real scientific experiment!

2. Keep a tortoise, wood turtle, or box turtle in your backyard inside a fence for at least two months, and describe in your notebook

its daily habits and what it eats. Determine also how far it travels about each day and how active it is. Can you get it to feed from your hands? Does it become affectionate and friendly at all from careful handling? Does it beg for food? Make a pool big enough for it to swim in and see if it does any swimming. Don't try this with a tortoise as this creature has no interest in swimming.

3. Keep one of the swift-swimming turtles, such as a cooter, slider, or soft shell, and its mate in a swimming pool or a large aquarium where you can watch its swimming ability. Time the swimming speed and see what is its fastest speed. Some turtles have peculiar methods of courting their mates; for example, the male may have a long nail on its foot with which it caresses the female when swimming. Describe in your notes how this is used. If you can put fish into the pool, see how the soft-shelled turtles catch these fish.

4. Tortoises do a lot of digging usually to stay away from cold or heat and where they can spend days sleeping. If a tortoise from the desert or plains is in your backyard and begins digging a hole, time it with a stopwatch, if possible. Use a long stick to see how deep it has dug to determine the exact speed of its digging. Compare this with another tortoise or another kind of turtle.

5. Test the intelligence of a tortoise, wood turtle, or box turtle in finding food in a maze. With turtles, a maze does not have to be very high, probably foot-high boards or aluminum plates with wooden stakes to hold them are enough. Increase the intricacy of your maze as the turtle gets more accustomed to it. Compare how long it takes different turtles to find food in the maze.

6. Observe how different kinds of turtles and tortoises react to and escape from danger. The box turtle, for example, closes doors in front and back of its body so that it is so tightly shut that hardly any animal can get at what is inside the box. But some animals, like a fox or wildcat, may try to fool the turtle into opening its box. What does the turtle do to prevent this? Act like a fox yourself and see.

Musk or stink-pot turtles of the East and Midwest give off a bad smell that makes an animal thinking of attacking them stop because they feel these animals will also taste bad. How effective is this defense on *you* when you pick up one of these turtles? Soft-shelled turtles usually escape an enemy by great speed and swiftly turning to bite. Watch in a pond and see if you can see one of these turtles making an escape like this.

Stink-pot and loggerhead musk turtles climb high up on the limbs of trees overhanging the water in order to sun themselves. This is probably to escape larger turtles or creatures like alligators that might try to seize them at the water's edge. But there is another very good reason. If something like a snake, for example, tries to climb up to get them, all they have to do is fall straight down into the water to get away quickly. This is a trick these species must have developed over a long period of time and shows one of the survivals of the fittest.

Try to find other such tricks of survival among the turtles and tortoises. For example, the snapping turtle and alligator snapping turtle have such fierce big heads with powerful snapping jaws that almost no one wants to attack them head on. The snapping turtle ferociously attacks whenever it is attacked.

7. I think you could have a lot of fun with a turtle race or tortoise race as long as you treat the animals with respect. Do not injure them, and let them go when the game is over. You can use the same aluminum-walled racetrack described for lizards (Figure 7–4) although the walls can be lower since turtles and tortoises cannot jump as high as lizards. Time their different speeds and see which species of turtles are the fastest.

ADVENTURES WITH INSECTS AND SPIDERS

9

Capturing and Keeping
Live Insects

MANY INSECTS ARE most active at night, especially after hot summer days, and so some of these very interesting creatures are not often seen by human beings. It is especially vital for all of us to get to know those insects that are destructive to our crops and stored foods, and also those insects and birds that hunt down these destructive creatures and keep them from getting too numerous. Almost all spiders, which are not insects but related eight-legged arthropods, are helpful to us in this way and should be welcomed to our gardens instead of destroyed. Daylight insects are usually most numerous after late spring rains followed by hot sunny days, and at those times can be easily captured or studied, especially along hedgerows, edges of woods, and places where flowers are numerous.

I want to emphasize very strongly that insects and spiders are living creatures with a certain amount of primitive intelligence and awareness. You can keep them in cages for a day or two or sometimes a few more for observations and experiments such as are suggested, but be sure they are well fed and watered, and let them go just as soon as you are finished with what you are doing with them. Be careful that they are not hurt or injured so they are released in good condition. If any do become crippled or otherwise injured, kill them as painlessly and as quickly as possible. If you cannot care properly for your insects, then it would be much better if you did not collect and keep them at all!

METHODS OF CAPTURING INSECTS

Different kinds of insects are most easily captured by different methods. Some can be caught in nets, others will come to traps, and still others are attracted by sugar baits.

Netting

Capturing insects during the day with butterfly nets requires some skill, which is gained by experience. Crash nets are made of canvas and are used for crashing through bushes to shake insects on the branches into the heavy net. These kinds of nets and how to make them are shown in Figure 9–1. I found from two years experience in the jungles of Panama that the best way to capture a butterfly or other flying insect is to sweep the net up behind it so the butterfly does not see the net coming. Otherwise, the butterfly can easily dodge it.

Stinging insects, like wasps and bees, need to be taken out of the net carefully by putting a jar over the insects and then placing a cap quickly on the jar. The cap should have holes punched in it so the insects can have enough air. On hot days, place a few drops of water on the leaves in the jar to help keep the insects alive. Cages and terrariums and how to make them are discussed later in this chapter.

Jar or Can Ground Traps

To make a ground trap, dig a hole in the ground near bushes, trees, rocks, or other places where insects congregate, and place a fair-sized jar or can in the hole (Figure 9–1). Tamp the earth around the jar so the top is just level with the ground. Next place a log, rock, or some other obstruction about one-half inch above the top of the jar or can on some smaller rocks or blocks of wood so there is still plenty of room for insects to find their way into the trap. The covering is to keep out

Figure 9–1. Capturing insects. (*a*) Pattern for buttefly net. Upper edge length equals hoop circumference. (*b*) 10-inch wire hoop attached to wooden handle with friction tape. (*c*) Detail of how wire hoop fits into grooves and holes in handle and how net is sewn to muslin strip around rim. (*d*) Using butterfly net. (*e*) Crash net made in same manner as butterfly net but with heavier materials and shorter handle. (*f*) Using crash net. (*g*) Cloth dipped in sugar mixture as bait. (*h*) Sugar mixture painted on tree. (*i*) Insect in ground trap baited with fruit.

rain water and to prevent dirt from being pushed into the jar or can by animals; it also keeps flying insects, such as beetles, from flying out of the trap. At the bottom of some traps, put an orange rind or a piece of peach; at the bottom of others, some old meat or fish. See what comes! Do not leave these buried cans or jars alone for more than twenty-four hours; otherwise your captured creatures may starve or become dessicated.

Beetles are the main creatures you will probably find entering these ground traps. They are, for the most part, perfectly harmless if you hold them in the middle so they cannot bite. Their bites are usually mechanical and not poisonous, but some ants do have poison in their jaws and can cause pain. Padded tweezers can be used for picking up many of these creatures and putting them in jars. Sometimes you may catch a mouse, which you will want to release unharmed.

When you are through using a jar or can in a particular location, be sure to move it to a new collecting site or discard it. Do not leave it as a trap where insects will fall in and then die by hunger or thirst.

Black-light Traps

Black-light traps have been used very effectively by the U.S. Department of Agriculture in fighting insect pests and in finding out when different insects fly at night.

The black-light trap possibly can be bought at some grange co-op store or it is fairly easy to build your own. A baffle-type black-light trap is shown in Figure 9–2. It is constructed as follows: Make a screen cage 12 inches by 12 inches by 12 inches, with a plywood top. Cut a hole 3½ inches in diameter in the top. Place in the hole a 15-inch-long galvanized tin funnel that is 3 inches wide at the bottom and 12 inches wide at the top. Firmly wire the funnel to the four corners of the cage. Place two wooden crossbeams at right angles to make a bridge over the top of the funnel which then supports four 10-inch-high galvanized tin baffles to reflect the light. Fix a black-light bulb in a socket mounted in the center of the crossarms facing up between the baffles. (If 6-inch black-light bulbs are to be used, then use 8-inch-high baffles, instead of 10-inch ones.)

I suggest you use the 9-inch, 6-watt F6TS-BLB G.E. lamp, which can be ordered from a lighting dealer. You will also need a starter condenser, other fixtures, and a ballast transformer. Figure 9–2 shows

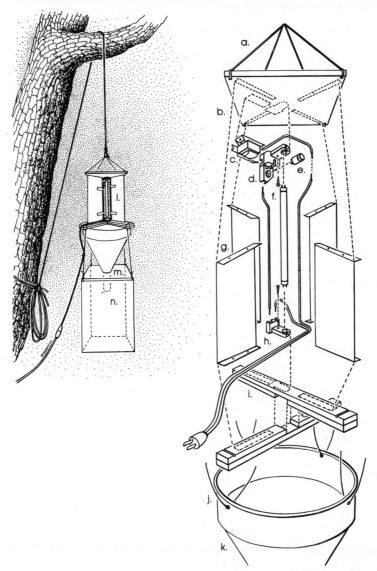

Figure 9–2. How to make a black-light insect trap. (*a*) Wire or cord. (*b*) Plywood top, 10 by 10 inches. (*c*) Ballast transformer. (*d*) Bracket for black-light bulb and starter condenser. (*e*) Starter condenser. (*f*) 9-inch black-light bulb. (*g*) Baffles made from galvanized tin or aluminum flashing. (*h*) Black-light bracket. (*i*) Wooden cross braces. (*j*) Wire ties. (*k*) Funnel, 12-inch diameter, 15 inches long. (*l*) Electrical wires taped to baffles. (*m*) Plywood top tied to funnel with wires. (*n*) Screen cage, 12 by 12 by 16 inches.

how to wire the starter and transformer parallel to the bulb with one lead from the end of the bulb and another from the ballast transformer strung to the electric wall plug in your house or shed. Place and fasten the starter condenser and the ballast transformer to the plywood top as indicated in the diagram. All wiring that is outdoors and all connections should be waterproofed with waterproof rubber tape. Warning: Do not look at one of these lights too long as they give off partly ultraviolet light and may give you a headache.

Sugar Baits

Many insects that are not attracted to light traps or are unlikely to be trapped by jars or cans in the ground are attracted to sugar baits. The best kind of sugar bait is a combination of fermented and mashed fruit such as bananas, apricots, and apples, plus molasses or thick syrup and stale beer. This mixture is heated and mixed thoroughly together, then carried in pails or jars as you go through the woods, orchards, or parkland. It should have a mild fermented odor. You can use an old paint brush to paint the mixture right on tree bark, or you can dip a rag into the mixture and tie it to a branch or the side of a tree with string or wire (Figure 12–1). Insects attracted by the bait are then captured in a jar with a lid that has holes in it.

Some day-flying butterflies, moths, and other insects come to this sugar bait by day, while night-flying insects come at night. Many become so intoxicated with the food offered that you can readily pick them up and put them in your jars or cans, each with a cover filled with holes for air. The catocala moths that come to the bait at night are especially spectacular and beautiful. Their hind wings are beautifully striped with different colors, while the upper wings are dark mottled to look like bark. As the moth flies, it shows the bright markings of its under wings; but, if a bat or other night creature tries to attack it, it immediately folds the camouflaging upper wings over the bright-colored lower wings and lands on some bark, seeming to disappear as if by magic.

IDENTIFYING INSECTS

For your observations and experiments to mean much you need to correctly identify the species of insects you collect. Good books to help you do this are listed in the References at the end of this book.

However, the number of different species of insects, spiders, and their relatives is so tremendous that even in North America alone there are tens of thousands of kinds. Some books produced many years ago are now out-of-date because many of the scientific names have been changed. For example Essig's *Insects of Western North America* badly needs to be revised; although a much later book, *Insects of California* is very helpful, it is entirely too small to cover adequately the many species of insects in this one state alone.

Another problem is that while some insects can be identified readily from pictures, others can be identified down to species only by using a magnifying glass to carefully study small differences in the wings and legs or in the reproductive organs. Whenever you are not sure of the names of some insects, phone or write to the nearest biology department of a college, university, or museum and ask if you can bring or send specimens for identification. These specimens, mounted correctly on pins, should have the correct date and exact location where each has been found to be any good to the scientist. You should send duplicates so the scientist can keep examples of different species as payment for his or her help.

KILLING AND MOUNTING INSECTS

I no longer kill and mount insects because I do not have the reasons for doing so that I had in the past; but, it sometimes is necessary when one is studying insects to do this so that the different live species can be properly identified.

An effective and safe killing jar (Figure 9–3) can be made by pouring about two inches of a thick creamy mixture of plaster of paris into a pint or quart jar, letting it dry thoroughly, and then pouring about one inch of ethyl acetate (obtainable at most drug stores) on top of the dry plaster of paris. Leave overnight and pour off the excess the next morning. Cut out three or four round pieces of blotting paper to fit the jar and press these down on top of the acetate and plaster of paris. Insects placed in this jar will die comparatively painlessly within a few minutes.

The outside of the killing jar, especially the bottom, should be reinforced with tape to reduce the risk of its breaking. All killing jars should be labeled, "POISON."

While you are collecting in the field, captured insects can be placed in hand-folded or regular envelopes, which will help protect them from

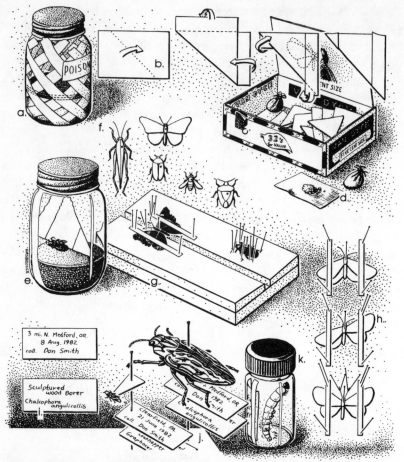

Figure 9–3. Killing and temporary storage of insects: (*a*) **killing jar;** (*b*) **storage envelope made from folded paper;** (*c*) **temporary storage box;** (*d*) **packet of moth crystals made from cheesecloth and string. Mounting insects:** (*e*) **relaxing jar;** (*f*) **pinning diagram;** (*g*) **mounting board made of styrofoam or corrugated cardboard;** (*h*) **wing-setting diagram. Labeling insects;** (*i*) **insect labels;** (*j*) **pinned and labeled insects;** (*k*) **labeled insect preserved in alcohol.**

damage (Figure 9–3). Always record the date and location of capture on the envelope before putting the specimen inside. The insects can be mounted later that day or temporarily stored in these envelopes until a convenient time for mounting. When insect specimens are stored, a packet of moth crystals should be placed within the storage container to prevent damage by dermestid beetles.

If, as often happens, you temporarily store killed specimens without mounting them, you can prepare the stiff, hard, stored specimens for mounting by putting them into a can or jar filled with damp sand on the bottom, which is covered with blotting paper (Figure 9–3). Leave the specimens in this "relaxing" jar for a few days to soften. A few drops of carbolic acid put in the sand will prevent the dampness from growing mold on the specimens.

After death, insects can be mounted as shown in Figure 9–3, with each one carefully labeled. It is best to use special insect pins for mounting. These pins are longer, thinner, and sharper than regular sewing pins. For general use, sizes #1, #2, and #3 are best, depending on the size of the insect being mounted. I use #2 most of all. Insect pins can be purchased at hobby stores or biological supply houses, such as Ward's Natural Science Establishment, 3000 Ridge Road East, Rochester, N.Y. 14622; Ann Arbor Biological Center, 6780 Jackson Road, Ann Arbor, Mich. 48103; Carolina Biological Supply Co., 2700 York Road, Burlington, N.C. 17215; or California Biological Service, 1612 West Glendale Blvd., Glendale, Calif. 91201.

After mounting, the specimens are put in cigar boxes or something similar with cork or celotex glued to the bottom (Figure 9–4). They can then be taken to experts for identification, or you can try to identify them yourself from books. Once identified, the proper common and scientific names should be put on the labels as shown in Figure 9–3.

Some very soft-bodied insects (especially larvae) and spiders may not be able to be mounted in this way. They should be placed in labeled jars or bottles with either 30% formaldehyde or 70% alcohol. If you use alcohol you have to begin first with a 70% solution and gradually add more over three to four days to finally make a 90% solution, as otherwise the specimens become too brittle. (Note: formaldehyde is a dangerous chemical; handle it with great care!)

Besides labeling your specimens with the correct names, it is a good idea to describe in your notes the habitat where each specimen was found and the exact location. This will make your collection more interesting and useful to scientists. For example, you might write in your notes along with the species name, "South slope of Mt. Saint Helena, California; 3,000 feet, in manzanita-chamise-ceanothus chaparral; May 4, 1982."

EXPERIMENTS WITH BLACK-LIGHT TRAPS

1. Hang the light trap in front of a large white sheet tacked on a wall or over a large window. Count how many insects come to the trap

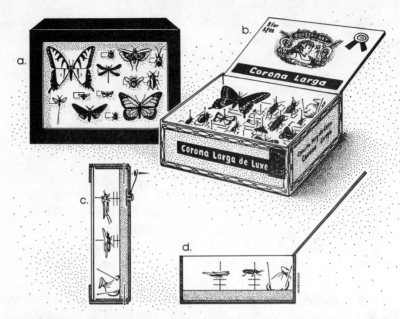

Figure 9–4. Storage boxes for mounted and labeled insects. (*a*) Storage box made from cardboard carton and glass. (*b*) Storage box made from cigar box. (*c*) Cross section of (*a*) showing glass glued inside of cutout top, with celotex, cork, or styrofoam on bottom, and with two brass paper fasteners (one shown) and string so that box can be hung on wall. Lid of carton is pinned to the bottom. (*d*) Cross section of (*b*) with pinning material on bottom. Moth crystal packets are placed inside storage boxes to protect specimens.

and how many to the sheet. Keep records for several nights. What are the most numerous kinds of insects in each place? To test the power of the sheet still further put a special light either in front of it or in back of it. Count how many insects come and how this compares to the black-light trap. The sheet may actually draw more insects than will be caught in the trap.

2. Fix the black-light trap so it can be pulled by rope and pulley high up in a tree or fixed at medium heights. Each night put the light at a different height and see whether you are getting different kinds and numbers of insects at the different altitudes.

3. If you can afford more black-light traps, put several at different places in your backyard or frontyard—one near thick bushes, another under a heavily foliaged tree, another in an open space where there is grass. Keep careful notes of all your captures at all designated places

to see what difference the different habitats make in the kinds and numbers of your catches.

4. Try your black-light traps at different hours of the night. Turn the lights on only during the experimental hours; for example, one light for from 8–11 P.M., another from 11 P.M. to 2 A.M., and another from 2–5 A.M. Describe in your notes all the differences you notice in the kinds and numbers of insects that come to the traps during each time.

5. By monitoring insects throughout a whole summer or during spring, summer, and fall, you can learn if certain pest insects are becoming numerous in your area. You can contact your nearest County Department of Agriculture, or state, or U.S. government offices so they become aware of this. If you discover a pest in your trap that has not yet been discovered in your area, this information will be extremely vital to your neighborhood agriculture office. Ask them for advice, too, on what to look for.

6. Humidity along with temperature may have a great deal to do with which kinds of insects come to your traps and in what numbers because different insects are adapted in different ways to different humidities and different temperatures. To keep a scientific record of the changes of humidity and temperature in your neighborhood would be a great help in this project. If you have the proper instruments and take measurements every four or eight hours, you can compare these records with the quantity and kinds of insects caught in the traps and begin to see a pattern in their flights that tells a great deal about their lives.

You can construct your own wet and dry bulb thermometers for determining humidity. Mount two ordinary thermometers on the same piece of plyboard (Figure 9–5). Tightly tie a wick of cotton cloth on the bulb of one thermometer with some thread. Next, attach nylon cord to the plyboard so that the plyboard with its two thermometers can be swung in a circle at high speed, which you do after thoroughly wetting the wick in water. After about a minute of whirling this sling psychrometer, as it is called, read the temperature in both the wet and dry bulb. Write down your findings in your notebook. Now get a psychrometric table from the U.S. Government Printing Office in Washington, D.C., and use this table to determine the relative humidity at the time you made the two readings. Double thermometers that give relative humidity temperatures without having to swing them are often available at local grange co-op stores or other hardware stores.

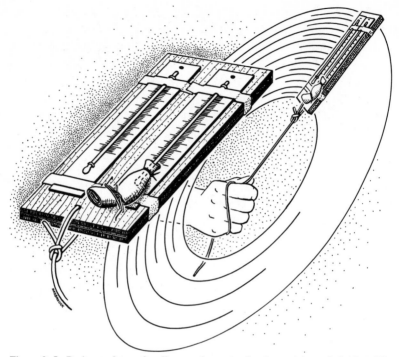

Figure 9–5. Design and use of a sling psychrometer for determining relative humidity.

MAKING CAGES, TERRARIUMS, AND AQUARIUMS

Insects and spiders can be housed in comfortable habitat cages or terrariums (Figures 9–6 and 9–7). The key is to make the surroundings as much as possible like that the insects would find in the wild. Examples of a woodland habitat, desert habitat, and pond habitat are shown in Figure 9–7. Other types could be brushy habitat, rocky habitat, and grassland habitat. Cages are covered with wire netting except for a wooden roof and floor, and each has a door. Smaller cages could have a sliding glass window to make the inhabitants easier to see. Terrariums have glass on three or four sides and wire netting on top which can be lifted up to get at the interior, change water or food, and clean up. Watching the creatures in these habitat cages or terrariums makes it far easier to observe their habits and tricks than it is in the wild.

The two great rules, however, that will be followed by every decent

Figure 9–6. Sample insect cages. *Front to back:* **large jar with holes in the lid; milk carton with plastic or celluloid walls and top (with holes); cardboard box with plastic, glass, or celluloid walls and screen top; wooden box with glass top, screened opening for ventilation, and glass front glued to wood with a silicon sealer.**

human being are to (1) keep your cages, terrariums, and aquariums clean and well supplied with food and water at all times, and (2) let all your animals free into the wild where you caught them as soon as you no longer have any interest in watching and studying them. The only exception to this second rule would be if you were keeping some creatures, such as boll weevils or tent caterpillars that are harmful to farm or garden life. When you no longer want to study these harmful creatures, destroy them as quickly and humanely as possible. For information about what to feed captive insects, refer to books that describe the particular types you have.

Figure 9–7. Examples of terrarium and aquarium habitats. *Top to bottom:* desert habitat; woodland habitat; pond habitat.

EXPERIMENTS WITH INSECTS IN CAGES OR TERRARIUMS

In all scientific experiments remember to treat your captives with kindness and do not subject them to pain or unreasonable discomfort. In many ways they have feelings just as we do.

1. Water insects, such as water boatmen, water striders, toad bugs, backswimmers, water scorpions, diving beetles, damselflies and dragonflies and their larvae, all have different ways of finding food and escaping enemies. Do not overcrowd your pond terrarium at first; just

have a few of these creatures in the water section. Watch them carefully over several days and then draw a diagram that shows their relationships to each other and their methods of escape from enemies (Figure 9–8). One by one add new creatures that you bring from the nearest pond to the terrarium, and watch how the newcomers affect and are affected by the other denizens of the pond and its shore. Draw in the proper connections as shown in the diagram. What are the most dramatic changes as different insects are added and what creatures become dominant in the pond?

2. To collect small creatures to feed to your captive insects in a woodland habitat, gather some leaf mold and dead leaf litter from a nearby woods. Place this in a large funnel that is inserted into a large jar with damp blotting paper in the bottom. Then shine a light on the funnel contents to cause the tiny creatures in the leaf mold to move into the jar (Figure 9–9).

Now place this living food into your woodland terrarium and watch how quickly the larger inhabitants such as ground beetles, rove beetles, lacewing flies, snake flies, baby mantids, and other predators go after this largesse of food. Their success as hunters is based on how fast they detect such food and how quickly they get to it before another predator does. Make a diagram on a sheet of paper as you are watching the hunting and draw lines for each hunter's attack. How quickly or slowly does it go about reaching its quarry?

It is exciting to investigate the life history of one kind of insect predator such as a mantid or mantispid or a tiger beetle. Watch and diagram and describe all the ways it has to catch its prey. Study ways the different kinds of prey insects try to escape or hide from the predator with camouflage. You can also diagram food chains in which you show how a frog eats a mantis, a mantis eats a wasp, a wasp eats a fly, and a fly parasitizes a wasp or another fly, and somewhere in the food chain a creature eats a plant, which is the beginning of most food chains. Diagram different food chains and escape routes as you find them in the terrarium. (See Figure 9–8 for an example.)

3. Let loose into your woodland terrarium all the flying insects you catch one night in a black-light trap. As these creatures fly around in the terrarium at night you can watch them with a flashlight whose light is covered with red plastic so only red light comes out. (Red light is hardly noticed by most denizens of the night; whereas, a white light would cause many to go into hiding. In this way, you can watch the

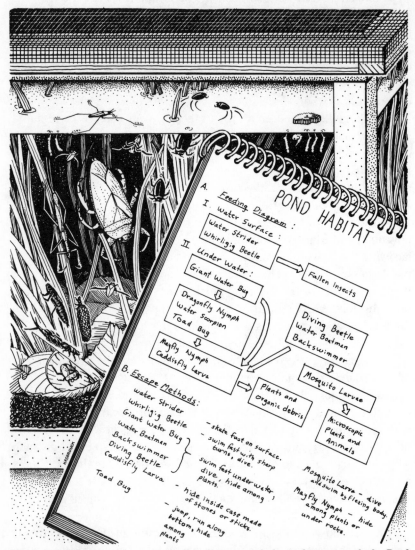

The handwritten chart in the illustration reads:

A. Feeding Diagram:

I. Water Surface:
Water Strider
Whirligig Beetle

II. Under Water:
Giant Water Bug

Dragonfly Nymph
Water Scorpion
Toad Bug

Mayfly Nymph
Caddisfly Larva

Fallen Insects

Diving Beetle
Water Boatman
Backswimmer

Mosquito Larvae

Plants and Organic debris

Microscopic Plants and Animals

POND HABITAT

B. Escape Methods:

Water Strider
Whirligig Beetle — skate fast on surface.
Giant Water Bug — swim fast with sharp turns, dive.
Water Boatman
Backswimmer
Diving Beetle — swim fast under water, dive, hide among plants.
Caddisfly Larva — hide inside case made of stones or sticks.

Toad Bug — jump, run along bottom, hide among plants

Mosquito Larva — dive and swim by flexing body.
Mayfly Nymph — hide among plants or under rocks.

Figure 9–8. Pond aquarium with feeding diagram and chart of escape methods. Pond insects, *left to right:* on water surface—water strider, whirligig beetles, mosquito egg; just below surface—mosquito larvae, water boatman, backswimmer, diving beetle, mosquito larvae and pupa; mid-water—water scorpion, giant diving bug, diving beetle; near bottom—mayfly nymph (*in foreground*), dragonfly nymph; caddisfly larva with case, water boatman; on bottom—toad bug. An actual aquarium should not be so crowded.

Figure 9–9. A method of collecting live food for insect terrariums.

night happenings of a woodland night in your own home.) Again, diagrams should be made and notes taken about what you see happening.

Many night-flying insects are seeking mates. Do they find them and mate with them in your terrarium? If so, do you see any eggs produced as a result of these matings? How are the eggs protected from enemies? The mantis, for example, covers its eggs with a foam that hardens into a fine protective barrier against enemies, while other insects hide their eggs in cracks in tree trunks or rocks or camouflage them so they cannot be seen. Watch carefully and your knowledge of the woods at night will greatly increase.

4. One of the marvelous aspects of insect life is *insect metamorphosis,* a marked and more or less abrupt change(s) in structure as the insect matures. Insects can be grouped according to whether they undergo no, incomplete, or complete metamorphosis.

Very simple insects such as the primitive insects of the subclass Apterygota do not metamorphose. Most are wingless and they grow from egg to adult in a straight line with no different forms along the route. Most familiar of these are the bristletails and the silverfish (which are not fish at all). The springtails are easily told by the forked spring on their rear that enables them to jump three to four inches and by their way of living in damp leaf mold in forests. The silverfish are found in most houses crawling up walls and sometimes feeding on old books. Put some of these creatures into a jar with proper habitat and watch them lay eggs and grow from tiny youth to adulthood without any changes.

Examples of insects that undergo incomplete metamorphosis are the milkweed bug, katydid, and cricket. Put several of these into a small terrarium and see that they are fed with proper food—grass for the grasshopper and milkweed for the milkweed bug. See how they lay eggs and how these develop into tiny creatures like the parents, but without wings. The wings appear in the final stage after the last molt, so these insects are said to have incomplete metamorphosis.

An example of complete metamorphosis occurs in the common western parsley swallowtail butterfly that can be kept in a few pairs in a large jar with parsley leaves. After mating, eggs are laid on the cabbage and these hatch into worms or caterpillars, totally different from the adults. The little worms gradually grow into big worms and then form into the pupae or chrysalid in which they are dormant for many days. At last, out of the chrysalid comes the butterfly, bedraggled of wings at first, but gradually taking shape until it forms a totally different appearing butterfly.

10

The Incredible Ants

ANTS ARE EASY to find almost anywhere. Plenty of them build their nests or towns in cities, in backyards, or even in homes, especially in places in a cellar where there is some dampness, but not too much. Out in the country they are found in practically any kind of habitat you can think of from dry desert to thick forest, avoiding only places where there is too much water or ice.

Because they live far longer than most other insects, sometimes seven, eight, or even ten years, ants have a much longer time to gain experience and even learn to make choices that show at least a rudimentary form of intelligence. This makes them very fascinating to watch and explore. Some build cities with thousands of inhabitants, many specialized for different kinds of jobs in their cities, as we are in our cities. Scientists are not sure whether an actual intelligence runs such a city, but it is an amazing structure to explore.

Since ants do not fly, except when the young queens and kings prepare to rise into the sky to mate, a butterfly net to catch them is not needed except at that time. (See Figure 9–1 for how to make a net.) Ordinarily, if you are careful, you can pick up most ants with your fingers. Some like the fire ants have fiery bites and some have stings like wasps. You had better use padded tweezers to pick up such ants. Be sure to do it carefully so you do not hurt the ants.

MAKING ARTIFICIAL ANT NESTS

Different kinds of artificial ant nests, or cities, can be easily made. These are very useful in studying how ants live and for testing their ability to learn and show intelligence.

Figure 10–1 shows how a simple nest is made in a jar in which dirt from the original ant nest is placed. The jar has small holes in its top to let in air, and you can place food and water on top of the dirt. This kind of nest is good only for small ants, but they soon dig holes down through the dirt and eventually make rooms where they store their eggs and their pupae, and a big room where their queen lays the eggs. The queen is usually larger than the other ants and must be found and put into the nest if it is to be successful. Handle her with special care.

A more useful nest is shown in the center of Figure 10–1. This is made of two pieces of glass held close together in a board frame (say, 10 by 16 inches so the glass is about ⅜ to ¾ of an inch apart. This allows you to watch the ants digging and using their tunnels and rooms in the dirt. Most of the time the glass should be covered with a thin cardboard or with black paper so the ants in their passages and rooms are in darkness, which is natural underground and makes them feel protected. In the top of the nest you put a damp sponge from which the ants can get moisture; keep the sponge damp by dropping water on it every day. You can also put food in the top part of the nest through a hole plugged with cork. (Refer to next section to determine what food to give them.) You can remove the side boards or black paper when you want to watch the ants at their city activities, but keep it off only long enough to make the necessary observations, putting the covers back on whenever you are sure you are finished.

You can make an attachment to the ant city (Figure 10–1d) that allows the ants to wander about and hunt for food. This gives you a chance to experiment with them to see how and when they may exhibit what seems to be intelligence in their actions. This extension is made from a flat plyboard about 18 by 24 inches, with walls a few inches high. It is covered with a glass or top. Small wood partitions are used

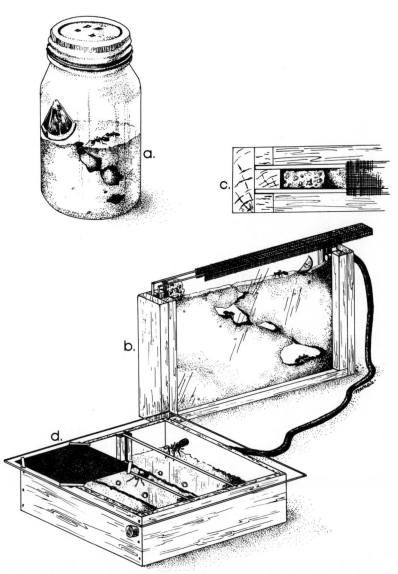

Figure 10–1. Artificial ant nests. (*a*) Jar nest. (*b*) Two-sided nest with glass panels. (*c*) Top view of two-sided nest showing damp sponge that provides moisture. (*d*) Ant city extension attached to main nest with plastic tubing.

to divide up the inside; these have holes bored in them for the ants to pass through. The wood parts should be painted with varnish two or three times to make them waterproof. The walls can be made of plaster of paris, instead of pieces of wood.

A plastic tube or tubes (⅜ to ½ inches in diameter) connects the dirt-filled nest to this extension so the ants can go to and from their main nest by way of the tube or tubes. Some of the rooms on the board can be covered with dark paper so the ants can keep their larvae or cows (aphids) in such places, while the rest are left open for the ants to forage in. A cork plug or two should be put at one end so you can add an extension or even another ant colony for testing two kinds of ants against each other. At these extension holes it would also be possible to put barriers such as deep channels between colonies or foraging rooms to test the ants' abilities to overcome difficulties. Such holes also enable you to give more room to expand to a growing ant colony or city.

DIGGING AND CAPTURING NESTS

When digging up an ant nest you will probably need more than just your hands. A trowel may be necessary for digging small nests, while digging large ant cities, such as those of the leaf-carrying ants of the Southwest, may require a pick and shovel, also.

It is necessary to get down deep enough into the city to find the queen, who is always larger than the other ants. You can lay a piece of cloth (at least 2 by 2 feet) on the ground near the nest, and pour dirt loaded with ants onto this cloth. As you dig down to find the ant underground chambers, watch very carefully for the queen. Pick her up with padded tweezers when you find her and put her into a small jar with a little dirt and a few other ants.

If you cut around the upper part of the ant nest with your trowel or shovel, sometimes you can pry up a kind of cap of hard earth on top in such a way that you can see how the tunnels and rooms are arranged underneath. This will help you find the queen much easier, as well as the eggs and the larvae and pupae that you will want to move very carefully to your artificial nest. While you are digging you should have your pants legs tied around the top of your shoes with strings so the ants cannot crawl up under your clothes. Keep brushing them off your clothes so they cannot bite you.

BEHAVIOR OF DIFFERENT ANTS

You can find ant nests almost anywhere except in water, extremely cold places, or in extreme rocky and sandy deserts where there are practically no plants. But special kinds of ants like special places. Some of the ant species found in the United States are illustrated in Figure 10–2.

The big black carpenter ants (*Camponotus*) are found wherever there is dead wood such as a dead tree, a dead stump, or a fallen log and are found practically all over North America where it is not too cold. You may need to make two artificial ant nests for them, one with dirt between the glass panes and the other with a sheet of wood through which you can watch them gnaw their tunnels. Besides wood, carpenter ants also love sweets of all kinds and are pugnacious about taking such things from other ants or insects.

One very interesting ant found in the woods in clearings of most of the mountains of the eastern states is *Formica exsectoides,* the large mound-building *Formica* ant which is distinguished from other ants by the wide grooves on the back of its head. It constructs large mounds, two to three feet wide and one to two feet high, out of earth and vegetable debris. It is also noted for capturing the pupae of the timid *Formica fusca subsericea* (⅖ inch long; silky shiny black; legs dull red or brown) and using the ants that emerge as slaves. Putting a nest of the latter ants near the former in your private artificial nests will soon show you how this is done.

Found all over the country in brushy areas, but in the West usually under sagebrush, is the red and black enslaving ant, *Formica sanguinea.* It forms armies to march into the territory of the timid *Formica fusca* (the common brown *Formica* ant), overwhelming these lesser ants and capturing their pupae and larvae to turn into slaves. You can watch this whole process by connecting two artificial colonies of these two kinds of ants by plastic tubes. *Formica fusca* is noted for its densely hairy body.

A still more interesting ant found in many parts of North America, though rarer in the West, is the shining amazon or slave-making ant, *Polyergus licidus,* and *P. rufsscens,* the western species. It is some-

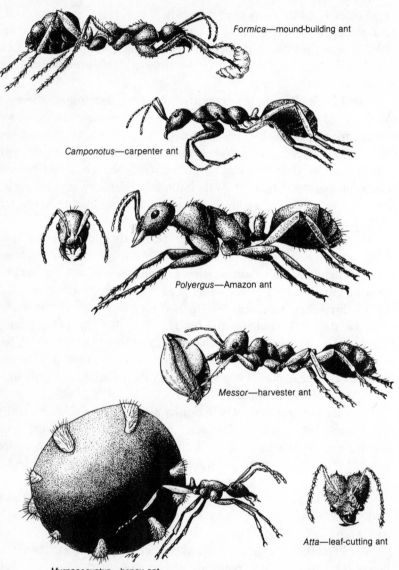

Formica—mound-building ant

Camponotus—carpenter ant

Polyergus—Amazon ant

Messor—harvester ant

Atta—leaf-cutting ant

Myrnecocystus—honey ant

Figure 10–2. Various ant species found in the United States.

times a beautiful shining red-brown all over, and is particularly noted for its ice-tong-like jaws that are made for piercing the skulls of other ants, especially *Formica rufa,* the common brown ant. The amazon ant cannot feed its own young because of the lethal shape of its jaws. So it marches in armies against the cities of *F. rufa,* where it kills any workers that resist and captures the pupae and larger larvae, which it takes home to its own nest to act as slaves. If you make artificial nests for both these kinds of ants and connect them with a plastic tube, you can watch this process of enslavement.

From Texas to Colorado and west to the dryer southern parts of California can be found the *Myrnecocystus* or honey ants, which generally live in sandy areas with sandy craters for entrances to their nests. When you dig down to their underground chambers you encounter many ants hanging upside down from the roofs, each with its belly so distended that it looks like a large, round, dull yellowish pea. These expanded stomachs hold clear liquid nectar that other ants have brought to these "honey pots." The honey dew is collected from aphids and other honey dew insects by the workers in the springtime and stored in the "honey pot ants" as vital food to be used during the hot, dry seasons of the year. The Mexican Indians used these as "candy." If you can get these ants into an artificial nest, you can watch how the honey pots are filled. Handle them with care, as they are fragile.

From Kansas and Texas to the Pacific Coast in dry areas are many kinds of harvester ants of the genera *Messor* and *Pogonomyrmex.* These ants are usually black, black and red, or all red and have powerful jaws for cracking seeds. They also usually have rather potent stings and so should be handled very carefully. Found in Texas and also farther east are other harvester ants of the genus *Pheidole,* which have prominent lobes on the sides of their heads. Most of these harvester ants can be told by the large mounds of fine sandy earth they make about their craters or holes, some mounds being as much as two feet high and nine feet wide. Usually, these mounds are cleared of all plants by the ants who also make trails or roads through the grass out to where they find the seeds.

All sorts of experiments can be done with harvester ants either in their natural settings or in large artificial nests. The following are suggestions:

1. Build bridges across water or deep ditches and see how long it takes the ants to find these bridges and use them.

2. Count the seeds the ants bring in for storage during a four-week period of dry weather. Then estimate how many seeds they might be expected to gather for winter storage during the warm part of the year.

3. In an artificial nest give the ants different kinds of seeds on different days. See which are most popular, and study the habits of an outside nest to find out why.

4. Bring strange ants into the nest of harvester ants and see how they and the other ants react. Get these strange ants identified by species at a local college biology department, if possible, so you can give the actual name of each kind of ant and write down how it reacts and how the harvester ants react to it.

The fungus or leaf-cutting ant, *Atta* (or *Cyphomyrmex*) is usually reddish in color, and is found only in the Southwest. They are noted for their angular heads shaped something like an arrowhead with prongs on the back. They climb trees and bushes to cut off small pieces of the leaves and carry them down into the nest where they are used as mulch for growing beds of yellow fungus on which the ants and their larvae feed. Some make immense nests or cities of tens of thousands of ants. To watch them in your artificial ant nest raising their food like farmers should be a fascinating experience. You can try different kinds of fresh leaves to see which ones the ants like. See how they make roads to the trees.

Just as exciting are the army or driver ants (*Eciton*) also found in the Southwest, but also in the lower southern states. In the United States they do not produce the immense armies of millions sometimes found in the true tropics; nevertheless, in this country they do form columns that march through thick vegetation rounding up insects they meet and tearing them to pieces with their large curved jaws. It is amazing to see army ants surround a large grasshopper, caterpillar, or spider and tear it to pieces in a few seconds. They also attack the cities of other ants, destroying the workers and carrying off the young and pupae to be used as food.

It is more fun to follow an army ant column for most of a day and observe what it does than to try to put these ants into an artificial nest (although this might be possible if you captured a queen). Usually there are large officer ants that seem to direct the efforts of these armies. Put most of these into jars and see what happens to the columns of lesser ants. In the columns themselves, watch the officer ants closely. Do they seem to direct the columns in any way? Do they get more respect and attention than the other ants? Put barriers in the way of the army ant columns. Do the officers seem to give commands about this? I have seen such officers appear to call for help when they get in danger. I have also seen them rush and lead the way to attack large and dangerous insects, spiders, or scorpions. See what you can find out about this!

11

Amazing Antlions

THE ORDER NEUROPTERA, or net-veined insects, includes many interesting creatures, such as lacewings, mantid flies, and owl flies, but the most amazing of all are the antlions. Antlion adults have the usual net-wings with a specially large border of cross veins on the fore part of the front wings, and they look very much like damselflies although their method of flight is more clumsy and slow. The wings do not seem to coordinate very well when they fly. Their soft and very long bodies measure around 1 ¾ inches, and their wingspan is about 2½ inches. Most of them drink nectar from flowers or nibble on pollen; some eat nothing at all, simply living long enough to mate and then leave eggs buried in sandy ground.

It is the larvae of antlions, however, that are most unusual. They have quite large heads at the end of a flat and soft body, but their sickle-shaped, long, spiny jaws are made for killing small insects. Some of them simply crawl around under the surface of sandy or sandy-loam soil, coming to the surface to seize passing insects. The most remarkable larvae are those that dig round conical pits and lie in wait at the bottom of these pits for ants or other creatures to fall into them

(Figure 11–1). The antlion makes these pits by working around in a circle throwing up sand and dirt with its shovel-shaped head until a smooth, well-rounded pit is formed. Their heads are about ⅜ to ½ inch long, but their neck muscles must be extraordinarily strong, as they may throw up small rocks as high as twenty inches into the air. One scientist studied the matter closely enough to figure that an antlion he watched threw a small rock so high that it would be equivalent to a strong man throwing a 25-pound rock 550 feet into the sky.

Whenever an ant or other insect starts slipping into an antlion pit, the antlion usually responds by throwing up sand and pebbles to force the ant into the bottom of the pit where the antlion seizes the prey with its long, strong jaws and then sucks the fluids out of its body. Each jaw or tooth has a deep groove in it which carries the ant's body liquids into the antlion's mouth. Once caught in those sharp and powerful jaws, few ants or other insects can escape. The antlion, however, buries itself in the sandy soil below its pit if too large a creature gets into the pit.

EXPERIMENTING WITH ANTS AND ANTLIONS

I described in Chapter 10 how to make artificial ant nests, or cities, and how to extend the range of these cities into other areas by running

Figure 11–1. Antlion larva capturing an ant.

a plastic tube from one box to another. To study how antlions interact with ants and other insects in the wild, you can connect an ant nest to another box with a plastic lid in which antlion larvae have been placed in sandy loam soil (Figure 11–2). This box should be at least 12 inches wide by 18 inches long and filled with sandy loam to about 4 inches. Leave a 4-inch space above the sand, and place a piece of glass or plastic on top to keep the ants from escaping.

This arrangement provides a natural way to study what ants and antlions do under natural conditions, without forcing any insects into

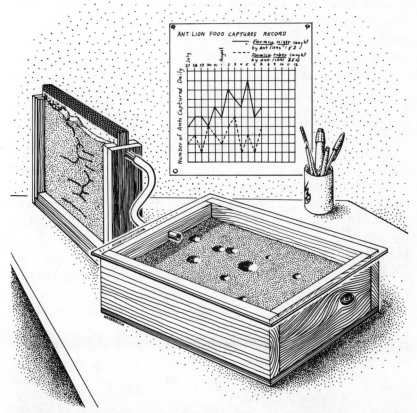

Figure 11–2. Flat antlion box containing sandy soil connected to two-sided ant nest. This experimental arrangement can be used to study the ant-capturing ability of antlions. Graph the results as shown. Remove the glass or plastic top from the antlion box immediately after the experiment so the antlions have air. Antlions will remain in the sand even without a top if they have food regularly. If the antlions pupate, a screen top can be added so the emerging adults will not fly away.

the antlions' traps, which is hardly fair. After this is all set up comes the time to take notes on what happens. Record on graphs how successful the antlions are in capturing ants and how successful different ants are in escaping from the antlions (Figure 11–2). Perhaps you could even have two different species of ants connected to the antlion box at different times so you can discover whether one kind of ant is more clever or powerful than another and so escapes more easily from the antlions'· traps.

You can also number each of the antlion pits on a map of the box. Keep records of how successful each antlion is in capturing prey over periods of one or two hours in which you carefully watch all activities. You can, of course, experiment with other insects, placing them in the box either separately or at the same time as when you let the ants into the antlion box. The graph illustrates how different records can be made over a period of a month to give scientific evidence of the behavior of all the creatures involved.

TESTING THE STRENGTH OF ANTLION THROWING

In this experiment you shut out all the ant nests from the antlion box and rig a series of strings around and above the box that will indicate heights above the box. Place the strings at about 1- or 1¼-inch intervals above the box as shown in Figure 11–3. Then drop a pebble of the same exact weight as a BB shot into an antlion pit marking the number of the pit down in your notes. (Refer to Chapter 12 for a method of weighing small rocks.) Usually an antlion is annoyed when a pebble gets in his way of seizing an insect, and he tosses it out with a quick upthrow of his head. Watch carefully how high it flies, noting which of the strings it reaches on its highest thrust. Suppose, for example, that an antlion that weighs 1 gram and is 1.5 centimeters long throws a small rock that weighs ½ gram as high as a string that is 30 centimeters above the pit where the head of the antlion is situated. What would be the strength of the antlion compared to a man who is 6-feet tall and weighs 200 pounds?

Since the antlion throws the rock twenty times higher than its length, this would be equivalent to the man throwing a 100-pound weight 120 feet into the air, and we know that is utterly impossible. If a man of 200 pounds could toss a 100-pound sack of cement even 5

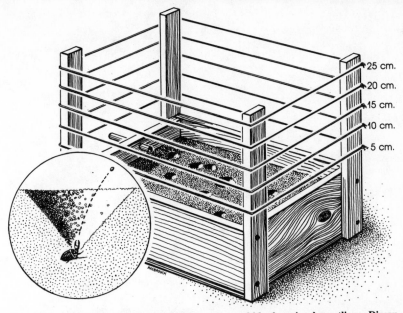

25 cm.

20 cm.

15 cm.

10 cm.

5 cm.

Figure 11–3. Experimental arrangement for testing pebble throwing by antlions. Disconnect antlion box from ant nest, attach posts to corners, and rig strings at intervals of 1 inch or so. Remove top and drop small pebble into antlion pit. Insert shows cross section of antlion pit with antlion larva tossing pebble.

feet in the air, it would be remarkable indeed. This experiment suggests that an antlion is at least twenty-four times as strong as a strong man!

Why don't you test several antlions with pebbles of different weights and see how high they can throw them. Keep careful records of all this. Also try to identify which species each antlion belongs to by showing your specimens, both larvae and adults, to an entomologist at the nearest college or museum biology department. Perhaps you can even measure the strength of two or more different species of antlions, if they are available in your neighborhood.

12

Testing the Strength
of Insects

MANY KINDS OF insects are capable of pulling or lifting extraordinary weights in comparison to their own weights and to what a man or horse could pull or lift. Trying to find out how much different species of insects can pull or lift is a fascinating project, but it must be done with care and thoughtfulness so as not to harm or give pain to the insect in any way. If you are not willing to exercise the kind of care necessary to insure that the insect at the end of the experiment will be in as good shape and health as when you began the experiment, then please do not try any of these experiments.

For these experiments, use only those insects that are encased in hard chitin (armored) covering such as most beetles, ants, and large bugs of the hemiptera type, or large orthopterans such as grasshoppers, stick insects, and jerusalem crickets. Leave the soft-bodied insects alone as they are too delicate and could not lift much anyway.

Dr. Ross E. Hutchins has experimented with different insects and has observed some herculean insect feats. For example, he saw an ant of the *Pogomyrmex* genus lift a stone weighing fifty-two times its own weight. A man to equal this would have to raise up nearly four tons.

This ant, however, did much less than the beetle that was seen to lift a weight 850 times its own weight. A man would have to lift sixty-two tons to equal this! By your experiments you, too, can test other examples of insect strength.

It has been found that insect muscles are not intrinsically stronger than those of human beings and other vertebrates, but the way they are attached to the walls of exoskeletons of the insects' bodies makes the insects' use of their muscles much more efficient than ours. Grasshopper leg muscles, for example, are about forty times more efficient than ours because of this positioning. One extensor muscle in a grasshopper generates in the act of jumping about 20,000 grams per gram of muscle while a human muscle generates in an athlete around 2,000 grams per gram of muscle. Quite a difference!

TEST EQUIPMENT AND PROCEDURE

When putting a harness onto an insect (Figure 12–1), it is necessary to use a soft thread that will not cut through the insect's exoskeleton and so hurt the insect. The thread should be snug but not so tight it cannot be easily cut off with a scissors when the experiment is finished. Use a slip knot for making the loops that fit around the body; one end would go back through a screw eye. The insect can be released by pulling the loose end of the slip knot.

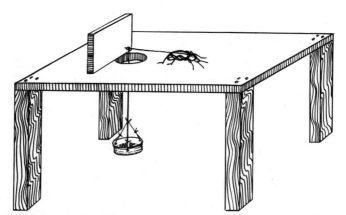

Figure 12–1. Insect weight-pulling experiment. Top of table should be rough so that insect will have traction.

Figure 12–1 shows the crude table with a hole bored at one end that can be used for testing the weight-lifting and pulling power of an insect. The exact weight of BB shots needs to be determined as shown in Figure 12–2. At a drugstore you can probably have the druggist weigh a BB shot on his scale so you will know its exact weight. You can then use different numbers of BB shots in your homemade scale to determine the weights that the insects you experiment with are pulling or lifting. Your scale should be so well balanced that the pans in each end, when not loaded, will equal each other perfectly. If the BB shots prove too heavy to get very exact weights of the insects in your experiments, use beads of exactly the same size each for finer measurements. Thus, you could find how many of the beads it would take to exactly equal the weight of one BB shot and so weigh an insect more accurately. If it is necessary to put an insect into a small vial while weighing it to keep it from jumping off of the pan, be sure to weigh the vial separately and subtract its weight from that of the insect and vial together.

Remember that the druggist, with the aid of his scales, will have given you the exact weight in grams or parts of a gram of one BB shot and also of ten BB shots for greater comparison. The main thing in the experiments is to know as closely as possible how many times the weight that the insect is pulling is in comparison to the weight of the insect. You can keep adding BB shots and then, if needed, small beads

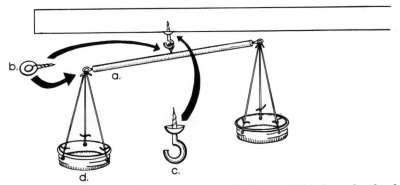

Figure 12–2. A homemade scale for weighing small objects. (*a*) ⅜-inch wooden dowel. (*b*) Screw eyes attached to dowel ends and to precise center of dowel. (*c*) Cuphook screwed into underside of shelf or table to support scale assembly. (*d*) Jar lid with three holes to receive strings that support lid.

until you find the maximum weight it can pull or lift. *Do not try to force the insect to do pulling or lifting that is beyond its capabilities.*

Be as careful as possible to be accurate in all your weighings so the records of these experiments will have actual scientific value. You probably should have a special notebook in which all these records are carefully kept; also note the date(s), time and place, and the exact name of the insect (common and scientific). Some of the more common insects you may be able to identify correctly from books on insects you get from libraries. The names of such books are given in the References section of this book. If you can't identify the insect yourself, show it to an entomologist at a nearby university or museum.

13

How They Can Jump!

THE JUMPING SPIDERS are usually small (⅛ to ½ inch or more) in size. They are noted for their quick movements and are among the most intelligent of spiders. They are found almost everywhere in the milder climate areas of North America.

To get to know these spiders under fairly natural conditions in your own home or on your porch, build or buy a terrarium about 18 inches or 24 inches long by 12 inches wide and 10 inches deep. Fill the bottom with sandy loam soil and place in it a few small plants taken from your garden until you have a tiny garden growing in your terrarium. The terrarium needs a wire-mesh top that fits over it in order to keep the spiders and their prey from jumping out.

Now look carefully for jumping spiders, all of which are also hunting other spiders. Sometimes you can encourage them with a stick to jump into a jar or box, or catch one with a small net and put it into a can. You know them by the quick movements and the long jumps they make, their short legs, their comparatively large and brilliant eyes, and their usually bright colors and short bodies. A jumping spider will turn quickly to face your finger if you bring it near, then suddenly jump away if you bring it too close.

Jumping spiders are found almost everywhere in gardens as they like flowering plants, but also can be found in deciduous woods, brushlands and, more rarely, in grasslands. They are daylight hunters and usually sleep at night. A few species copy ants in appearance and have unusually long bodies. Jumping spiders have no webs except the silky nests they make for their young. They can also spin a dragline to give protection when falling. When one is about to attack an insect, it approaches very slowly like a cat and then suddenly jumps or runs down the insect. Sometimes it catches its prey, sometimes not. If you can get a jumping spider into your garden terrarium and catch some grasshoppers, flies, plant bugs, and other prey to put in with it, you can watch how the jumping spider hunts and see some real tricks.

You can rig a system to find out how far different jumping spiders can jump. Some have been known to jump more than twenty times their length. Get a large sheet of heavy paper or of light cardboard and put a large dot in the center. Then draw concentric circles around the central dot with a felt pen, using a strip of cardboard with holes in it as a guide (Figure 13–1). Each circle should be a centimeter (about ⅖ inch) from the next one. These circles should extend out about 50 centimeters (20 inches) from the center. Attach either an artificial fly or a dead fly very carefully to a fine thread whose other end is attached to a thin stick you use like a fishing pole.

Gently capture a jumping spider and place it in a small jar or plastic tube. Have two pins ready, preferably with differently colored heads, and have another person use the pole and thread to place the dead or artificial fly on the board with the concentric rings about 13 to 14 centimeters from the central dot. Now remove the plug from the plastic tube and gently release the spider as close as you can to the central spot. Your friend should jiggle and move the fly on the end of the thread as if it were alive. When the spider jumps to seize it, measure the jump by placing one pin at the spot where the spider jumped from and one where it landed at the end of its jump. If you both have keen eyes, you should be able to do this fairly accurately.

The spiders used in this test should be identified either with a good book on the subject (see References at the end of this book) or by taking specimens to a local biologist at a college or museum.

Several jumps will be needed for each species to find out more

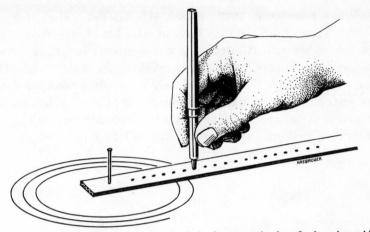

Figure 13–1. Method of drawing concentric circles for measuring how far jumping spiders can jump.

exactly its ability as a jumper. Record all your results on a chart to give a diagram of jumping spider's abilities in jumping. If you want to do this just for fun, why not have a spider-jumping contest with your friends like the famous Jumping Frog Contest of Angel's Camp, California. But, treat the spiders kindly and let them free when finished.

Another remarkable ability of jumping spiders is the habit of the males to court or "woo" their mates with some of the most fantastic signals and flashing colors in the whole animal kingdom. They mainly use their front pair of legs, but also sometimes the third pair, and occasionally other legs, the tops of their heads, and even their backs and bellies, showing off many colors, colored hairs, strange bumps, and other protuberances. They dance, pirouette, and use their legs to flash at the ladies complicated semaphore-like signals. Since the ladies are usually very coy, and sometimes actively hostile to these show-off males, the job of courtship is rarely an easy path. The beautifully decorated males often get in a frenzy in their attempts at courtship. Watching these antics in your terrarium, you can take some marvelous color photos of these activities if you have a close-up lens. At the very least you can use colored pens or pencils to make drawings of the more interesting signals and dances. The courting occurs most any time in late spring or early summer.

When a female is finally mated, you can put a drop of bright-colored, nontoxic paint on her body to mark her as an individual and then follow her actions in building a nest in your terrarium. Female jumping spiders not only lay eggs in envelope-like nests but guard the young spiderlings in the nest until they are ready to face the world. The nests have several silken envelopes so the young spiders are well protected. Some actually remain in those warm hidden nests all through the winter, apparently sleeping and waiting for spring.

14

Wonderful Spiders and Their Webs

I HAVE ALREADY discussed jumping spiders and their ability to jump long distances plus their intelligent-appearing actions. In this chapter, I deal mainly with the spiders that use webs in one way or another for catching prey. However, there is so much more to find out about their use of these webs and the silken lines they are made of, sometimes only a millionth of an inch in diameter, yet stronger by far by weight than steel, that a voluminous book could be written on the subject and be far from complete.

Think of just a few things spiders can do with their webs—net fish as a fisherman does, trap insects on the wing, lasso insects much larger than themselves as cowboys can a steer, form safe homes to block enemies from getting at them. Most amazing of all, perhaps, is the ability of many spider species to work into their web what may be a kind of sign language that talks silently to their mates, but which can also be read by their enemies and by humans if we can learn to place our minds where the spiders are. Probably a good majority of the 42,000 or more kinds of spiders in the world use this silken writing. I hope to show you how we may begin to understand this special language of spider webs and the function of webs.

Spiders' use of silk threads begins with the very simple one-thread rope, anchor, or lasso of the simpler hunting spiders, who may use one line, for example, of sticky thread to trap a small insect and then draw it in or track it down. This use extends on to the amazingly complex and beautiful great webs of the orb-weavers that sometimes fill the woods with astounding beauty when the dew of morning glistens on their lines (Figure 14-1).

I suggest you keep a special notebook on spiders, describing and drawing all your glimpses into the astounding lives of these creatures, so that you begin to have, after a time, not only a scientific interest in their history but a feeling that is almost mystical and spiritual, as if you were glimpsing somehow into the heart of all life. There is, indeed, nothing wrong with being at one and the same time a naturalist or scientist and one who feels the spiritual essence of nature. The writings of many great naturalists exhibit this dual approach to nature's wonders; for example, J. Henri Fabre and Colonel Laurens Van der Post, author of *The Heart of the Hunter, Jung and the Story of Our Time, Venture to the Interior,* and many other fine books. I use the word *glimpsing* above deliberately, for we humans are standing on the shore of a great Ocean of Truth, where, as Sir Isaac Newton, the famous physicist, once said, we see yet only a few beginning glimpses.

EQUIPMENT FOR STUDYING SPIDERS AND THEIR WEB LANGUAGES

The first tool you will need to study spiders is to overcome the foolish fear and disgust that so many people have toward spiders. View them, instead, as among the most intriguing and interesting of all creatures on earth.

The second tool would be *a good camera* that can take sharp color and black and white pictures, including close-ups of insects and spiders, as well as of the plants with which they interact. Spiders are very difficult to preserve as specimens and lose their beautiful colors very quickly if placed in formaldehyde or alcohol, which is why I recommend good sharp photos to use in identifying them. These photos can be used to compare with similar photos or drawings in good spider books, especially if the spiders are photographed close up. When you find it

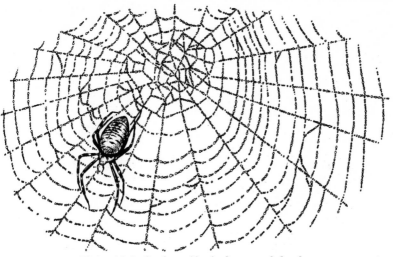

Figure 14–1. Garden spider in dew-spangled web.

difficult to get good photos in the wild, you may bring your spider or spiders to a good-sized terrarium filled with plants and rocks to be as natural looking as possible.

The third tool needed is a butterfly net made of good strong mesh like nylon, bobbinette, or green voile (Figure 9–1). Once a spider is swept into the net, especially a large spider, you need to use the utmost care to transfer it without injuring it to a large open-mouth jar with a thin metal lid that has been punctured with small holes to let in air. Open up the net carefully and place the open mouth of the jar over the spider so you do not have to handle it in any way. Then slide on the cover and you have a live specimen for your terrarium. The jar can actually be placed in the terrarium so the spider can crawl out; be sure that your terrarium has a tight wire-mesh lid on top so the spider cannot escape. At some later time when you are more expert, you may want to capture the two really dangerous spiders—the black widow and the brown recluse, or violin, spider (Figure 14–2), but at least the first year, you had better leave these two spiders strictly alone! All other spiders, including even the tarantula, ordinarily are not capable of doing you severe injury, though some are capable of giving painful bites. As long as you pass them from one place to another with the use of jars, there is little danger.

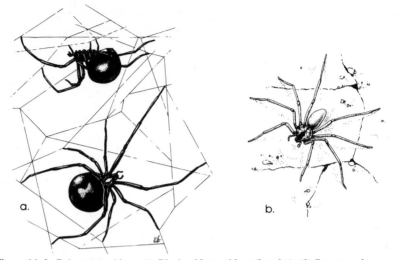

Figure 14–2. Poisonous spiders. (*a*) Black widow spiders (females). (*b*) Brown recluse, or violin, spider (note violin pattern running down center of cephalothorax).

The fourth tool you will need is either black or white spray paint (high-quality enamel paints are the best). This is to prepare spider webs for photographing them. Before you spray, however, remember you do not want to harm the spider; blow at it gently so it will leave the web.

You will also need a large package of colored construction paper, preferably both yellow and black, so you can use the black spray on the yellow paper and the white spray on the black paper. Finally, you need a can of clear-drying fixative spray, which gives you time to lift the web before it dries. (Fixative sprays are sold in art stores.) A good quality lacquer or enamel spray may be used instead, but is not as good.

PHOTOGRAPHING THE WEB

Make sure all approaches to the web are clear of brush and other obstructions. Hold the spray can about 10 to 12 inches away and then spray all parts of the web several times to make sure the design is distinct. Don't spray nearby plants if possible. Take a piece of construction paper a bit bigger than the web and spray this with the fixative spray until it's slightly wet. Place this carefully against the web until the web sticks to it. Break or cut all the spider's anchor lines so the web won't be torn, and then remove the paper with the web on it.

The two contrasting colors now bring out the appearance of the web as clearly as possible, and the paper with the web is ready for photography, which will be more permanent. Set up your photography equipment on a tripod wherever you feel you have the best light conditions. Put the web picture on a wall, focus carefully, and capture the design. For each web you photograph, you should also try to photograph the spider. This can be done either before preparing the web for photography or after the spider rebuilds its web. The spider can usually easily replace the complete web within a day.

STORING WEB PHOTOGRAPHS

The photograph of a web along with a photograph of the spider that built it should both be kept together in a special large box or file with each species both numbered and named. The paper with the affixed web also can be kept. If you cannot find the spider pictured in a book and identify it from a picture, send a copy of your spider photos to a nearby college, university, or museum entomology department after first asking them for permission to do this. Usually they will help you with identification, but especially if you send two copies of the photo of each species so they can keep one photo for their own files and send back the other to you with the name. For scientific work, the date and exact location of the photograph, plus details of the surrounding habitat, are necessary.

FORM AND FUNCTION OF DIFFERENT WEBS

It is important after you have photographed a web to come back the next dawn and watch the spider build a new web. This is often started just when daylight is beginning so you need to get up quite early to see the whole show. I assure you it is well worth the effort to watch an orb-weaver spider at work. It is really a tremendous job of engineering and can often be considered a work of art. Another reason for watching the spider build its web is to see if it gives you any keys to the function of the web.

My description here of an orb-weaver at work is very brief but sufficient to help you understand the basic engineering and design of an orb-weaver spider's web. It usually takes from twenty to sixty minutes to build a complete orb web depending on wind conditions. Too much wind, of course, may cause the spider to stop and wait for a better time. Remember the spider is working with a very intricate mechanism of up to seven glands in its rear end. These glands distribute liquid silk (all but invisible) to three pairs of spinnerets, which, along with the legs, act like fingers to spread the air-hardened silk lines where they are needed, the whole job being done by inherited instinct.

The first silken line is a dry one, without any stickiness to it, except that the spider may deposit a drop of stickiness to fasten ends where-ever it wants to. Often it has to get that first line across considerable space, such as between two separate trees or bushes, or even over a creek. To do this the spider climbs high on some branch, letting out behind it a single thread that is called the *dragline,* because such a line is generally dragged behind it wherever it crawls. This line, whose end is sticky, is hung down and allowed to drift on the breeze until the end hits and sticks to an opposite bush or tree. This becomes the *bridge line* and over it the spider goes, strengthening it with several more silken lines.

With the bridge line in place, the spider drops a second thread to another hold, pulls it tight and works a third across to form a basic triangle. After strengthening this triangle, the spider weaves a center, or hub in one part of it; this is where it will later sit, waiting for its prey. From this center the spider carefully begins to spread three dozen or so strands of dry thread like spokes of a wheel. A scaffold of dry thread is produced that makes the framework on which can be hung the vitally important and large outward-going spiral of sticky thread on which the insects the spider is waiting for will later find themselves enmeshed. This whole process is done by different species in different ways, some quite amazing. In the rest of this section, I will describe the main types of spider webs, hoping you will remember that there are many in-between types.

Single Lines

Only primitive spiders let out sticky single lines to trap prey. Feel-ing a tug on the dragline they have played out behind them, they rush back to find out and attack what they have captured. Often their prey escapes because a single sticky line is hardly enough to hold a strong insect.

Irregular Web or Net

Webs composed of a tangled mess of irregular threads are made by the comb-footed spiders, (Theredidae family) and are not as effective as the more sophisticated webs. (See Figure 14–3a). The common house spider, *Theridion tepidariorum,* weaves this kind of web, coming into the houses of humans perhaps because she cannot compete well with other spiders on the outside. The combs on the hind legs of these spiders are used to throw liquid sticky silk at insects and further enmesh them.

Sheet Web

Usually a fairly closely woven sheet is spread in a single flat plane, with threads running in all directions (Figure 14–3b). Members of the genus *Frontinella,* or sheet-web weavers, are most frequently seen making this type of nest. The sheet webbers often spin their webs across the faces of cliffs or in piles of rocks, under houses and other shelters.

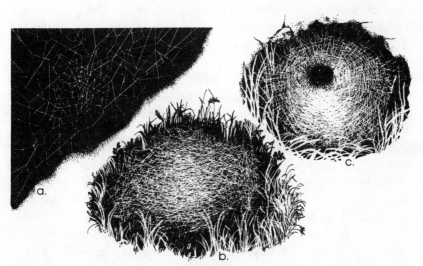

Figure 14–3. Some simple webs. (*a*) Irregular web or net. (*b*) Sheet web. (*c*) Funnel web.

Their webs are more organized than irregular webs. Sheet-web spiders dart across the sheets at high speed to entrap their prey.

Funnel Web

Funnel webs are simply sheet webs with tunnels attached (Figure 14–3c). These webs give their owners more protection against enemies than do simple sheet webs, especially when the tunnels lead into cracks in the rocks or between boards where large enemies cannot go. But the funnels may suggest that their builders are very timid spiders who want to be safe. The circle-eyed grass spider, *Agelena naevia,* makes this type of web.

Orb Web

There are several types of orb webs, but all have a sticky line placed in a spiral or part spiral going out from the center of the web and a framework of radiating lines that are not sticky.

Complete orb with meshed hub (Figure 14–4a). Usually in complete orbs the web is quite symmetrical, with the viscid line mainly in a beautiful spiral until it reaches the outer edge where it is often looped back and forth several times on the lower side of the web. The mesh at the hub is usually a combination of several irregular-shaped smaller meshes, and can be either rather open and thin or densely compact and quite strong-looking, almost like a seat of power and authority. The foliate spider, *Aranea frondosa,* spins a beautiful example of this kind of web.

Such orb webs are nearly perfect examples of web building and are extremely effective in catching prey. The large and beautifully colored spider often sits in the center of the web waiting like a magnificently decorated chief.

Complete orb with sheeted hub (Figure 14–4b). The sheeted hub, made of a densely woven sheet of spider silk, is spun over the network of the hub. *Argiope,* mostly large orb-weaver spiders, is a genus that commonly has this kind of web, with the banded garden spider, *Argiope trifascida,* a prime example.

Complete orb with open hub (Figure 14–4c). The simplest type of complete orb web resembles the hub of a wagon, but with a hole in the center. This kind of open hub is found in the webs of the Tetrag-

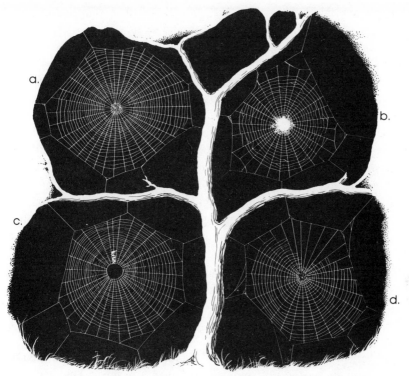

Figure 14–4. Types of orb webs. (*a*) Complete orb with meshed hub. (*b*) Complete orb with sheeted hub. (*c*) Complete orb with open hub. (*d*) Common incomplete orb.

nathinae subfamily and the genus *Micrathena*. The arrow-shaped orb-weaver spider, *Micrathena sagittata*, is a good example. Although the hole in the hub would seem to give prey a chance to escape, the real reason for this opening in the web is probably yet to be discovered.

    Common incomplete orb (Figure 14–4d). In incomplete orb webs, the viscid or sticky thread makes only a few spiral turns before it becomes looped back and forth on the radial lines, making an incomplete orb. Old spiders of the genus *Nephila* (strong thread-weavers) have few loops, while the young spiders have many more. Are the old ones getting tired or is there some other reason for their making such webs? The very long strong lines may make up for the lack of completeness. Hardly anything in insect life can escape those strong lines. The spotted-legged orb-weaver, *Nephila clavipes*, produces a fine example of this web. But how the loops of a common incomplete orb are arranged varies greatly among the different species. Why don't these

spiders complete the web with the spirals of the viscid thread? A lot
of watching and thinking may find the answer.

Domed orb (Figure 14–5a). Only one species, the domed-web spider (*Hetnztia basilica,),* makes domed orbs. First it completes an orb
web, then pulls it into a dome-shaped structure, presumably for better
protection from enemies. Perhaps other reasons for the dome can be
found by close observation.

Zygiella-type orb web (Figure 14–5b). The Zygiella spider leaves
a definite portion of the orb it builds without a viscid line, although
there is a trapline for escape, extending from the hub to a hiding place
above the web, and opposite the vacant section of the web. This kind
of web is produced not only by spiders of genus *Zygiella,* but also by
some of the spiders in the large genus *Aranea.* However, sometimes
a Zygiella spider will make a complete web, so the Zygiella-type web
is not totally specific to this genus. In the Zygiella-type web, another
feature is that the trapline or escape line usually goes upward from the
center and away from the vacant area of the web. Again we can guess
that the spider is leaving a sector of the web without sticky webbing
for some specific reason. Much watching and research may find an
explanation for this behavior.

Ray-formed orb web (Figure 14–5c). This unusual ray-formed orb
web is made by the ray spider, *Teridiosoma radiosa.* This web com-

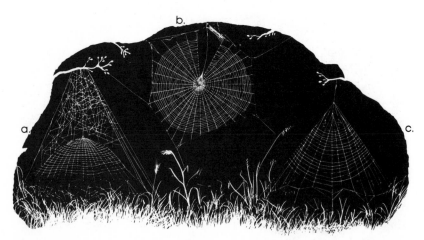

Figure 14–5. Types of orb webs. (*a*) **Domed orb.** (*b*) **Zygiella-type orb.** (*c*) **Ray-formed orb.**

pletely lacks a definite hub or center, but has radiating dry lines forming several (four or five) irregular rays or groups. The spider uses its dragline or trapline somehow to pull the whole web into a different shape such as a cone or funnel with the small end near where the spider is resting. If an insect is trapped on one of the sticky lines, the spider lets go of the trapline in such a way that the web springs open, ensnaring the insect even more in the sticky lines. Because of the closing up of the lines into a cone or funnel, about one-third of the web is left open without the viscid lines in it. Here, indeed, the spider seems to be inviting the victim into a clever trap. How did this kind of web ever get started, and what exactly is its function? Can you find out?

Triangular orb web (Figure 14–6a). The unique and beautiful triangular orb web is produced by the triangular spider, *Hyptiotes cavatus*, and the closely related species, *H. gertschi*. These tiny spiders, about ⅙ inch long, are so beautifully camouflaged like a brown twig that the only signs of their presence are the triangular webs. The web is made up of four strong lines radiating from one branch to another. The transverse lines and sticky lines have little humps on them of overlapping lobes that make them appear hackled (like *Uloborus* webs, see next section). These lines or bands appear somewhat zig-zag. Though it looks like just a fragment of an orb web, scientists claim it is really a complete orb. The radii or hackled bands vary greatly in number.

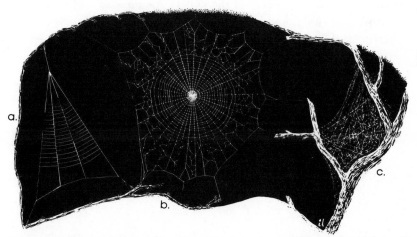

Figure 14–6. Types of orb webs. (*a*) Triangular orb. (*b*) Orb with hackled band. (*c*) Irregular orb with hackled band.

The spider usually rests and watches at the point of the triangle and so close to the twig it may appear as a part of it. Holding the line taut, the spider can snap it when an insect gets caught on a viscid line and keep snapping until the victim is thoroughly entangled. This sort of clever trapping should tell us a good deal about this spider and the functioning of its web.

Orb web with hackled band (Figure 14–6b). The usually complete orb webs of the genus *Uloborus,* or extended-legged spiders, are distinctive because the sticky threads have hackled lumpy bands, although these are generally not visible to the naked eye. The greatly extended legs of *Uloborus,* often twice the length of the body and other legs, are also distinctive. Another interesting item about these webs is that they are usually spun to form a nearly flat surface, generally with a mesh hub, and either complete or incomplete. Sometimes these spiders make many webs close together forming a colony. Perhaps some type of communication among the spiders occurs in such situations. Do the more powerful spiders, for example, have the more complete orb webs in the better localities for catching insects? Also, how are those very long front legs used for both signaling and for catching insects?

Irregular orb web with hackled bands (Figure 14–6c). These webs are produced mainly by the cribellate spiders, except for the genera *Hyptiotes* and *Uloborus.* These spiders include the Denopidae (ogre-faced spiders, because of their huge eyes, genus *Denopis*); the Amaurobidae (light-eyed spiders of the genera *Amaurobus* and *Callioplus*), and the Dictynidae (white- and dark-eyed spiders of such genera as *Dictyna* and *Scotylathys,* the six-eyed spider). All cribellate spiders

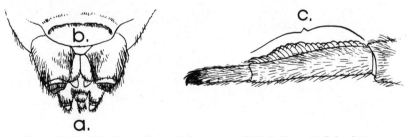

Figure 14–7. **Cribellate spiders.** (*a*) **Spinnerets.** (*b*) **Cribellum.** (*c*) **Calamistrum.**

differ from other families by having a *cribellum* (extra organ attached near the spinnerets) that produces through numerous spinning tubes the finest of all spider silk, and a *calamistrum* (a single or double series of dark spines along the tarsus of the black leg) that acts to make the hackled webs of these kinds of spiders (Figure 14–7).

Orb and Irregular Net Web

A complete orb web may be combined with an irregular net behind it into which the spider escapes (Figure 14–8a). Mainly spiders of the genus *Aranea* (typical orb-weavers) make this type of web. An especially interesting spider, the labyrinth spider (*Metapiera labyrinthea*), makes its orb and irregular net into a regular labyrinth in which it completely hides itself inside a kind of leaf tent. Perhaps these spiders are indicating that they don't trust an orb web alone for safety and want a net or labyrinth, also.

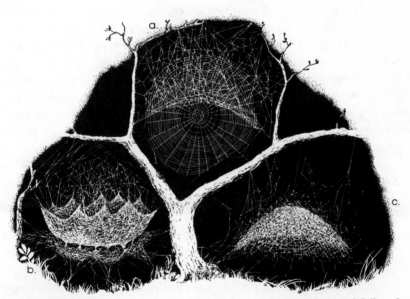

Figure 14–8. Combination webs. (*a*) Orb and irregular net web. (*b*) Bowl and doily web. (*c*) Filmy dome web.

Sheet and Irregular Net Webs

Sheet webs and irregular net webs were described earlier. The combination of these two types of webs can produce complex and exciting webs. The two best spiders to illustrate these are the bowl and doily spider, *Linyphia communis,* which produces above a flat sheet a filmy bowl in which it rests waiting for insects (Figure 14–8b) and the filmy dome spider, *Linyphia marginata,* which forms an exquisitely beautiful dome above a flat sheet, visible in good light against a dark background (Figure 14–8c). This spider waits just inside the dome top to pull insects that are caught through the wall. Examine these webs most closely and try to understand their function for the spiders.

Exploring, examining, photographing, and understanding the function of even a few of these fascinating webs could be a wonderful job. Why not try it?

MORE QUESTIONS ABOUT WEBS

As I've already noted, we are just beginning to understand the functions of webs and the purposes they serve for spiders. A few of the many questions that could be asked about spiders and their webs are suggested here as guides for your exploration of these creatures.

It is generally believed by scientists that the type of web a particular species of spider makes is an inherited characteristic; that is, the spider's ancestry dominates its web-building behavior. Nonetheless, close observation reveals some differences in the webs made by different individuals of the same species and even in different webs made by the same individual. You can look for such differences by photographing webs from several individuals of the same species, or by photographing several webs made at different times by the same individual, and examining the photographs carefully with a magnifying glass. Do you find some webs that show definite new characteristics or lack of old ones?

For example, an orb-weaver spider that usually creates a complete web may leave out part of the spiral in a particular web. Maybe the spider's inheritance permits some variation in web-building, perhaps in response to differences in its environment. Observe carefully where and in what circumstances spiders build their webs and you may see something that helps to explain differences in their webs.

If you examine a web closely and the actions of the spider that uses it, you can begin to understand the functions of the webs and how different spiders use them. For example, suppose a spider is trying to escape from a spider wasp that is trying to catch and sting it, either on the web or off it. Just how does the spider use the web and its different parts to escape? Observe different spiders of the same and different species to see how they act in a similar situation. Are there any things about the form of the web that help, or hinder, the spider in escaping from the wasp?

Spiders also exhibit differences in how they respond to large prey insects. A difficult creature to catch—for example, a large grasshopper, big wasp, or an assassin bug—would try the ability of a spider to handle safely and effectively. Sometimes spiders seem to actually be afraid of such creatures and cut them loose from the web. At other times, they act very quickly and effectively to make the catch and kill. Again, if you watch very carefully, you may observe some differences in the webs, the spiders, the prey, or the surrounding environment that help to explain these behavioral differences.

Write down in your notebook what your watching and testing and examining has shown, giving full details if possible. If you do this carefully and intelligently, making sure that you know the name of the species being watched and any other creatures involved, then you will be working like a scientist.

ADVENTURES IN DIFFERENT HABITATS

15

Tracking and Trail Finding

THERE ARE SEVERAL fine books about tracks and the trails they make in woods and fields and deserts. Some of these books are listed in the References at the end of this book. Look them up at your library. I am going to emphasize just one way of studying tracks because I think it brings about the most enjoyment and the most learning in the shortest possible time; but, I advise you to look up other ways in other books.

Every experienced tracker will tell you that learning to track an animal or even a man through woods and fields is not easy. It requires a very sharp eye and an intelligent understanding of what you see. If you go on to more detailed books on the subject and follow their directions, maybe you will become a real tracker, the mastery of which requires a great deal of hard work over a period of years. But with some comparatively simple equipment and techniques you can easily learn to see and understand what the average person never sees (Figure 15–1).

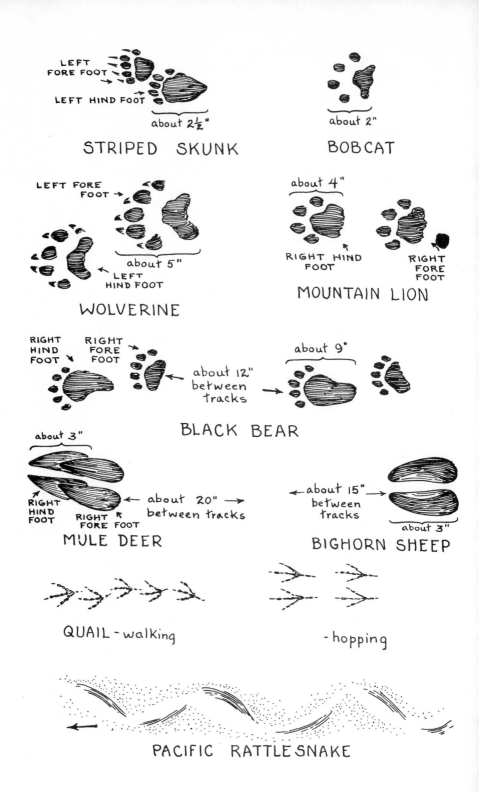

STRIPED SKUNK

LEFT FORE FOOT
LEFT HIND FOOT
about 2½"

BOBCAT

about 2"

WOLVERINE

LEFT FORE FOOT
about 5"
LEFT HIND FOOT

MOUNTAIN LION

about 4"
RIGHT HIND FOOT
RIGHT FORE FOOT

BLACK BEAR

RIGHT HIND FOOT
RIGHT FORE FOOT
about 12" between tracks
about 9"

MULE DEER

about 3"
RIGHT HIND FOOT
RIGHT FORE FOOT
about 20" between tracks

BIGHORN SHEEP

about 15" between tracks
about 3"

QUAIL - walking

- hopping

PACIFIC RATTLESNAKE

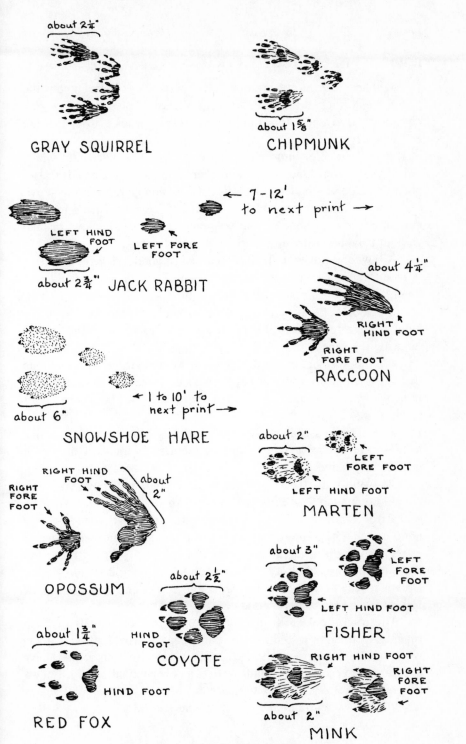

Figure 15–1. Tracks of various animals.

GRAY SQUIRREL — about 2¼"

CHIPMUNK — about 1⅝"

JACK RABBIT — LEFT HIND FOOT, LEFT FORE FOOT, about 2¾", ← 7–12' to next print →

RACCOON — about 4¼", RIGHT HIND FOOT, RIGHT FORE FOOT

SNOWSHOE HARE — about 6", ← 1 to 10' to next print →

MARTEN — about 2", LEFT FORE FOOT, LEFT HIND FOOT

OPOSSUM — RIGHT HIND FOOT, RIGHT FORE FOOT, about 2"

FISHER — about 3", LEFT FORE FOOT, LEFT HIND FOOT

COYOTE — about 2½", HIND FOOT

RED FOX — about 1¾", HIND FOOT

MINK — about 2", RIGHT HIND FOOT, RIGHT FORE FOOT

EQUIPMENT FOR STUDYING TRACKS

You need a good camera that takes sharp color or black and white pictures and a lens for taking close-up pictures. I also suggest a telephoto lens attachment for your camera to bring tracks closer that are at a distance.

If you use color film it is important to use a skylight filter which reduces too-strong blue tones where there are shadows. Consider, also, obtaining a polarizing lens that will cut down on glare from the snow.

A flat snowshoe or sandshoe (Figure 15–2) can be made to tie to the bottom of each shoe so that you can walk on sand, snow, or mud without leaving hardly any marks.

A bow and arrow with 80 to 100 feet of good nylon rope at least ⅜ inch thick is also needed. Rope tips can be made solid by burning them lightly with a match or candle until fused. The bow and arrow are for shooting the rope over a good strong limb in a tree; the arrow point is weighted so it will drop down with the arrow to the ground dragging the rope with it.

Various spray paints and perhaps powdered graphite in tubes can be used to carefully spray or paint tracks of animals so they stand out in snow, mud or sand. In mud, talcum powder can be used for this purpose.

A boatswain's chair with a shoulder sling can be hoisted up high in tree branches as a base for taking pictures of tracks, animals, or birds if they come.

To identify the tracks you see in mud, sand, and snow, you need a good book such as *Animal Tracks and Signs of North America,* by Richard P. Smith or others listed in the References. It would be wise not only to photograph the tracks but also to make your own drawings of them for help in identification and as a jog to your memory. Put these in your notebook identifying each and naming it (Figure 15–1). Drawings should be made of at least four tracks of any single animal or bird to be sure to get a good one.

The track books will usually picture tracks of animals or birds running, trotting, or walking so you can recognize what they were doing when the tracks were made. If the animal was running, it may have been trying to escape something or to run down and kill a prey. Follow the tracks carefully, and try to figure out what happened. Feathers or fur in the snow with blood will tell of a successful hunt.

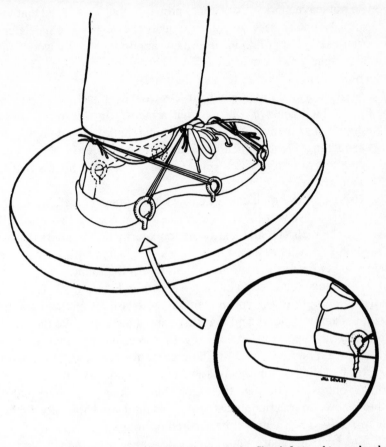

Figure 15–2. Sandshoe for walking without leaving tracks. Shoe is fastened to regular shoe by means of 1-inch screw eyes and laced with string. Close-up shows how underedge of sandshoe is rounded. Screw eye should not pierce through bottom of shoe.

PHOTOGRAPHING TRACKS

You can, of course, photograph tracks without any special preparation. But for good sharp photos in which the tracks stand out sharply, it is better to spray them with paint, graphite, or talcum powder to make them clear. Use colors that contrast best such as white on a dark background. Be sure to spray or paint so just the track is covered—nothing else. You may find a small fine brush will do the job best. Crouch on your makeshift snowshoes in the snow, mud, or sand so you do not leave marks. Locate and prepare enough tracks so that they tell stories—encounters with other animals or birds; attack and defense as when a skunk or porcupine uses its weapons of war, or a woodchuck turns to fight a fox when it cannot reach its hole in time. Dramatic adventures can indeed be told by the tracks.

I suggest you photograph the tracks from up in the trees if possible or from a high rock or cliff or even a ladder. In this way you can photograph a sequence of tracks, which can indicate a lot about what was happening. Plenty of people have photos or plaster-of-paris models of single tracks or a few in a small locality. The good photos that tell a story take time and effort.

Use the trees or a ladder or cliff with the utmost carefulness. That is why I suggest you have at least one and probably two good long nylon ropes with you and learn how to expertly tie the knots that will keep you safe. It is wise, also, to have a companion with you who can help you get up to the high places and return to ground safely.

The knots you need to know are shown in Figure 15–3. These will assist in your safety if you practice how to use all of them and use them correctly. Understand that there are some knots like the granny knot and the slip knot that are dangerous because they may give way when trusted and let you fall. The granny, for example, looks almost exactly like the reef or square knot, but does not have the two ropes coming out evenly through their loops but with one rope over and the other below. So practice tying these knots until you habitually do them all correctly. Then you will be assured of your safety.

The reef or square knot (Figure 15–3a) is used mainly for tying two ropes together that are of the same thickness or for knotting a single rope in a circle. The weaver's knot (Figure 15–3b) is used for tying two different types or sizes of ropes together, as it will not slip, and for tying the end knot of a woven basket or mat. The double or sheet-bend knot (Figure 15–3c) is also good for tying two different ropes together and is especially good for tying rope to a fish line. The rolling hitch with two half-hitches (Figure 15–3e) is especially strong and is used to attach a rope to a post or upright limb or trunk of a tree. The clove hitch (Figure 15–3g) has many uses and is very strong on a tree limb or post. To be absolutely safe, use a clove hitch combined with one or more half-hitches (Figure 15–3f). This should be used when you are hanging a boatswain's chair below with a swing. The bowline knot (Figure 15–3d) can be used to put a rope around your body so

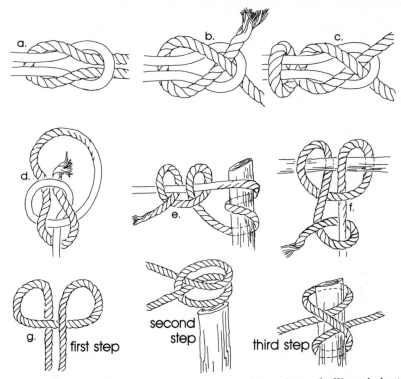

Figure 15–3. Useful knots for nature projects. *(a)* Square knot. *(b)* Weaver's knot. *(c)* Double or sheet-bend knot. *(d)* Bowline knot. *(e)* Rolling hitch fastened with two half-hitches. *(f)* Clove hitch fastened with half-hitch. *(g)* Steps in making clove hitch.

that the knot will not slip and start pinching you. Practice it often and carefully. This is put around your body as part of a sling to keep your body upright and absolutely under control so you cannot fall out of a boatswain's chair. The running bowline may be used to tie around a rock or for lassoing a horse.

I should remind you that if you use a ladder to climb up to take pictures of tracks, it is much better to use a three-legged ladder than a four-legged ladder, as a three-legged one has better balance. Even with a three-legged ladder, be very careful where you put the three feet of the ladder so they will not slip and cause you to fall.

To suspend the boatswain's chair (Figure 15–4), first shoot an arrow with an attached rope over a strong branch in a tree, if possible near where another branch will hold it. Then attach the sling rope (running from one side to the other of the boatswain's chair) to the tree rope with a weaver's knot, leaving an 8-to-10-foot tail. Loop the tail around your chest and secure it with a bowline knot. Now, you and your assistant both pull on the rope until you are high enough to have a good view of the ground where the tracks are. From this vantage point take several pictures of the tracks focusing as close as possible. The rope is anchored to the tree's base with a rolling hitch and two or even three half-hitches.

You need to be reminded here that while up in the tree in your boatswain's chair you may also get chances to focus your camera on birds or animals that do not realize you are there. This is especially true if you remain silent, move slowly, and keep your eyes open. Listen carefully as you may hear an animal or bird approaching before you actually see it and can freeze so it does not notice you as you get good pictures.

PROJECTS FOR STUDYING TRACKS

1. Watch for evidence in tracks of animals meeting each other; attacks by hunters on the hunted as a fox chasing and attacking a rabbit; birds coming to animal remains or something strange on the trail; courtship or mating behavior; two animals or birds playing with each other.

2. Watch for signs of running, trotting, or walking. Learn to differentiate these different ways of moving from the tracks.

3. Watch for signs of fights between males of the same species, shown in deer, for example, by hooves being driven deep into ground to leave deep tracks.

4. Night photos can be made with a camera attached to an automatic tripper that releases the flash and shutter at the same time when a deer or other animal trips a wire that has been placed across trail. The camera can be placed in a boatswain's chair positioned at the proper height over the trail.

5. Paint some tracks with phosphorescent paint so they will shine with light at night. Take photos of such shining tracks in the night from a ladder moved along to different parts of the trail. These should make very mysterious and beautiful photographs.

6. Place decaying meat or other offal from a carcass here and there along the trail. Take flash photos of animals that approach by setting up an automatically tripped camera in a boatswain's chair as described

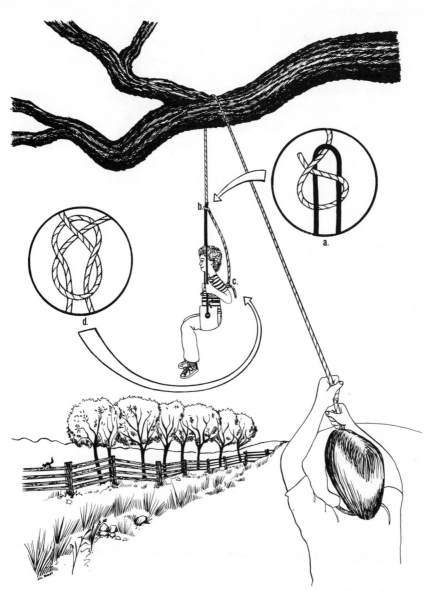

Figure 15-4. Suspending a boatswain's chair. The weaver's knot (*a*) attaches to the rope which supports the sling (*b*). The loose end coming out of the weaver's knot continues for 8 to 10 feet around the rider's body (*c*) and connects with a bowline knot (*d*).

above; or be up there in the night to take the photos yourself. Make photos of the tracks the following day to show who came.

7. Spread sand over an area where animals come and smooth it with a rake. Return in the early morning to take photos of tracks of animals that came to the area at night. Baits could be put there to lure more of them.

8. Experiment with getting close-up and magnified photos of insect and spider tracks by putting a very fine powdering substance on a flat area where a number of insects come. Photograph the area late in the afternoon when the low sun makes shadows of the tracks. Also attempt to get photos of the actual creatures that made the tracks so you can identify the track-makers. What do the tracks show the insects were doing? Examine the tracks carefully. Perhaps jumping spiders were hunting flies, or preying mantids were seeking grasshoppers, or ants were following a trail to good seeds for food.

16

Tree-Dwelling Mammals, Reptiles, Amphibians, and Insects

MAMMALS, REPTILES, AMPHIBIANS, and insects all have their own ways of acting in trees; generally they are very different from each other and from birds. With insects and amphibians (particularly tree salamanders), you usually do not need to hide in blinds. Tree frogs, however, are very aware of nearby human beings and will leap away to hide in dense bushes or even dive down into pools to escape your watching them. So, for tree frogs, as well as for mammals and reptiles, you generally need to have a blind where you can hide and watch them.

You want to make sure all the time that you or any friends who are climbing with you do so with the proper safety precautions (see Chapter 15). With children it may be necessary to use a harness with attached nylon ropes for anchoring the child to the tree in such a way that there is no danger of its falling. Although many children enjoy tree climbing do not force them if they seem unwilling. Even some adults are not comfortable above ground. For actually watching wild creatures, you need to make sure that children will be patient and quiet enough to be able to see interesting things.

Mammals, reptiles, and frogs may sometimes be watched from blinds if you are dressed in clothes that completely camouflage you by making you look like part of the tree. You also must remain perfectly still in one place for a long time. This is marvelous training in self-control. Clothes can be stained brown, yellowish brown, and greenish gray. Your clothes also need to be scented by rubbing them with a strong-smelling plant, such as sage, honeysuckle, mimosa, or bay leaf, to counter the human smell. Rub every bit of your clothes with the plant as well as your exposed legs, arms, and face.

The porcupine is one mammal you may see in the trees. This creature climbs trees, particularly pine and fir trees, to eat leaves and bark. It is slow moving and can be easily watched without bothering it too much if you are quiet. How it uses its quills to repel enemies is particularly interesting to observe.

The red squirrel of both eastern and western forests is extremely noisy and curious if it has not been shot at a lot. It makes all kinds of noises at creatures it thinks are interlopers and is very active running up and down tree branches and trunks, generally of conifers. It is rare in deciduous forests. See if you can observe red squirrels in courtship and raising young and how they escape enemies, particularly the marten.

Grey squirrels and fox squirrels are found mainly in eastern and western deciduous forests, though sometimes they venture into coniferous forests. There is much competition between them in the trees. Fox squirrels are generally more aggressive and noisy than grey squirrels though both become very quiet if they know a man with a gun or a wildcat is stalking them. Like most tree squirrels they keep their bodies on the opposite side of the trunk from you if they think you are dangerous. If you remain quiet a long time, they will gradually become curious or forget their fears and soon begin to act naturally. Try to watch them building their nests and raising their young.

The marten and the wildcat are the two worst enemies of tree squirrels. The marten lives almost entirely among the conifers and rarely comes into the deciduous woods to attack grey and fox squirrels. If either of these enter the conifers, however, they are much more easily caught by a marten than is the red squirrel. The reasons for this are that they are slower tree climbers, and their large size makes it difficult for them to hide in a hole too small for the marten, which the red squirrel often does. The competition or struggle between the red squirrel and the marten is a wonderful contest to watch. Sometimes the marten wins. Sometimes the red squirrel wins. As a last resort, a red squirrel will leap from a treetop down to the ground. Usually a marten is afraid to do this because of its weight. But, if the marten's mate is waiting below for the red squirrel, then it is too bad for the squirrel!

The wildcat has a more difficult time chasing tree squirrels than does the marten because it is heavier and cannot move quite as fast. I did see a wildcat one time, however, traveling through the treetops at high speed. The main way a wildcat catches a tree squirrel is by crouching silently among the leafy branches where it has hidden itself as carefully as possible and waiting there without moving until a squirrel comes near enough for it to leap and seize it. You would be extremely fortunate if you saw this happen.

Opossums also travel through the treetops, constantly investigating every nook and corner of the trees to see what they can find to eat. They are slower than tree squirrels, though I have seen one run along a branch quite rapidly. An opossum can use its tail, which is prehensile, for climbing and may even hang itself from a branch by its tail to watch what is going on down below. Because of its slow speed, the opossum has to depend on other methods to escape enemies. It gives off a bad smell that makes other creatures not very eager to kill and eat it, and it pretends that it is dead so that most animals leave it alone when in this state. It also snarls fiercely with its mouth wide open to show its formidable teeth, a tactic likely to give pause to other animals.

A mother possum has a pocket on her abdomen where she carries her newborn young for several weeks. Sometimes older young hang from the mothers' tail, while clutching her fur. Possums are omnivorous, eating almost anything, including dead animals.

Some ground squirrels climb trees, particularly the California ground squirrel and the rock squirrel of the intermountain West, but they usually run down a tree when they are frightened instead of rushing up a tree as does a tree squirrel. Some squirrels may attack salamanders, tree frogs, and lizards in trees and what happens when they do would be interesting to watch.

SUGGESTED PROJECTS

1. Get or make an artificial squirrel, and put it in a treetop where you can manipulate it with nylon fish lines as is explained with the owl dummy in Chapter 5. See what happens if a real squirrel comes near it to challenge it, or an owl, hawk, or marten to attack it.

2. Number the squirrels you meet or see when up in a tree in your notebook. With a stopwatch time the length of their calls and chattering. Also write down how many calls they make in different hour periods. Is there much difference between squirrels?

3. If you find a squirrel nest in a tree, get in a position up in a tree where you can watch the performance of the adults and the young using binoculars.

4. Make a census of all the snakes, lizards, frogs, and salamanders you find in trees or big bushes while you are in the trees. Describe in your notes their activities. Do the squirrels bother them or show any other interest in them?

5. Some creatures like snakes are usually up in trees and bushes to find bird eggs; others, like lizards, frogs, and salamanders, are there to hide from enemies. How successful are they? What other reasons can you think of or see for their being there?

6. A way to attract many of the animals discussed in this chapter to where you can watch them closely is to pound a four-foot stake into the ground so that the top just barely reaches the top of a small bush. Put an eye screw into the top of this and then nail a smaller stick to the upper side of the stake so it sticks above the stake about eight to ten inches. Put a smaller eye screw in the top of this, and then run an almost invisibly fine fish line through the two eye screws and attach one end of the line to a bright-colored feather, tying the fish line to the top of the feather, while the base of the feather is attached by string to the larger eye screw on top of the stake. Run the rest of the fish line out to a blind or other hiding place you have where you can sit and watch quietly while pulling the fish line every so often to make the feather jerk and flash in the air. This should make many animals and birds very curious and will bring them gradually near to see what is happening. Something similar could be fixed up in a tree.

17

Succession of Plants and Animals

ECOLOGY IS THE study of living things in relation to each other and to their environments. It is a fascinating study, but so complex that it is almost impossible for one person to grasp the whole of it. It is understood better as we see it in its parts, and one of the most interesting parts is what is called succession.

Succession refers to the ways plants and animals change as conditions change in their environment, some species dying or moving out and others coming to take their place. Primary succession occurs when plants gradually begin to grow on bare rock or bare mineral ground, ending after many centuries when the same area is covered by a forest of great trees. Secondary succession occurs when an area has its plants partially but not completely wiped out by a catastrophe such as a forest fire, and new plants (actually part of a higher stage in a primary succession) start growing where the great trees were before.

Steps in some kinds of successions can often be known in advance, but other forms of succession may vary greatly. Some successions are called partial successions because they either begin from higher stages of successions than is normal or because they end before reaching the final stage, which is called a climax. An example of a climax is a redwood forest on the Pacific Coast or a beech-maple forest in the East. In both cases, these are the largest trees that come to grow in a certain climatic area. Since they are the largest trees, they shade out other trees and become, in the end, the dominant trees, with only a few trees of lesser kinds remaining in their shade. This condition may last for many centuries until a great forest fire or lumbermen with their saws cause the destruction of the large dominant trees. Then a new succession begins.

In this chapter I describe how to study some simple forms of succession that do not take long to happen and to study food pyramids and food webs that also change along with the successions. A food pyramid is shown in Figure 17–1, and a simple food web is shown in Figure 17–2. Both are simplified to make them clearer to understand. You can build them even larger as you do your own experimenting and studying of life in the habitats that are found near your home. The main idea is to see what eats what and how the changing of a succession also changes the food pyramids, or chains, and the food webs in a given area.

SUCCESSION OF MICROSCOPIC LIFE IN WATER

A very simple experiment is to take some nearly pure water and observe with a microscope the creatures that appear over time. Get a large bowl or jar, fill it with water, and mix in a bit of hay or grass. Boil the mixture in a large pan. Allow it to cool and pour it back into your jar or bowl.

For this experiment you need a *microscope* that multiplies at least 100 times. A simple microscope of this kind is very inexpensive or can be borrowed. *Microscope slides* are needed for placing on the microscope platform and examining life. Get some *pine or balsam gum* for making rings on the microscopic slides in which you can put a small amount of water. *Cover slips,* thin glass squares, are placed over the water sample to keep it from evaporating too quickly. Figure 17–3 illustrates how to prepare a slide for examination under the microscope.

You begin daily, or at least every other day, to take water out of your jar or bowl; put it into a pine gum ring on a slide with a cover slip over it. Watch what you see in the water under your microscope.

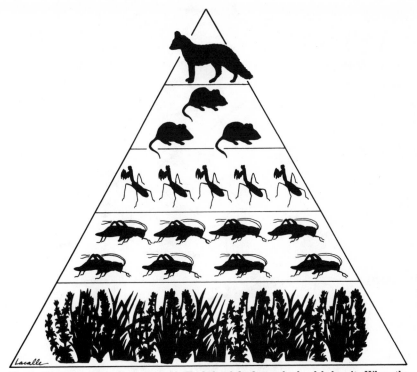

Figure 17–1. A simple food pyramid. Each level feeds on the level below it. When the animal at top dies, it decomposes into nutrients that support the lowest level in a never-ending cycle.

Either make drawings of what you see under the microscope or make photographs with a camera that can focus through the length of the microscope to which is attached a light to make everything in the water clear. Photographs must be taken in 1/100th of a second or less time to catch pictures of the creatures before they can move.

You will probably see something like the following stages of succession (Figure 17–4):

1. Spores of bacteria enter the water from the air, hay, or grass and begin to multiply rapidly. The clear fluid becomes milky as the acidity rises in the mixture. Other plants, such as algae, will begin to grow. This is called the pioneer stage of the succession.

2. Flagellates are early protozoans to enter the water, feeding on

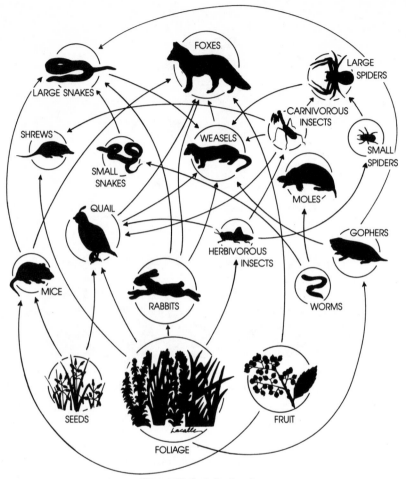

Figure 17–2. A food web.

bacteria and increasing rapidly. But numerous bacteria also remain. Flagellates usually have one or more long whiplike attachments (flagella), that thrash the water and drive them forward.

3. Colpodans (usually kidney shaped) become more numerous as the flagellates decrease, but some bacteria and flagellates are still present. Colpodans, such as *Colpoda campyla,* have tiny cilia (or hairlike projections) all along their sides to drive them like oars through the water.

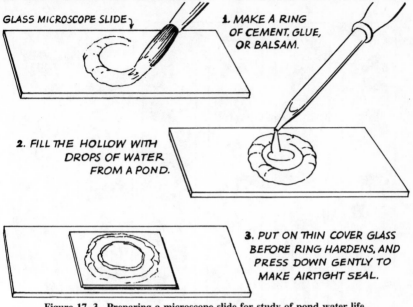

GLASS MICROSCOPE SLIDE

1. MAKE A RING OF CEMENT, GLUE, OR BALSAM.

2. FILL THE HOLLOW WITH DROPS OF WATER FROM A POND.

3. PUT ON THIN COVER GLASS BEFORE RING HARDENS, AND PRESS DOWN GENTLY TO MAKE AIRTIGHT SEAL.

Figure 17–3. Preparing a microscope slide for study of pond water life.

4. Hypotrichs, creatures with fused groups of short cilia formed in curves on the body, become numerous as the colpodans decrease. One good example of these is *Eschaneustyla brachytona*, which has a beardlike front end.

5. Parameciums, with their many tiny oars (cilia), and more rapid movements, appear now and gradually take over from the hypotrichs. *Paramecium caudatum* is the most common species. It is armed with many stinging hairs for attack or defense. The extremely interesting stalked *Vorticella* (with ciliate oars set like in a whirlpool) also may appear in this stage, as well as amoebas, whose moving fingers of protoplasm extend before them.

6. At the climax stage all creatures come in to balance in the habitat or microcosm, with green algae forming the basic food supply, while rotifers (truly astonishing microscopic or near-microscopic many-celled creatures with rotating whorls of cilia), copedpods, and amoebas become dominant.

As all these different characters appear on the scene, watch carefully and see who eats whom, and how each tries to escape enemies,

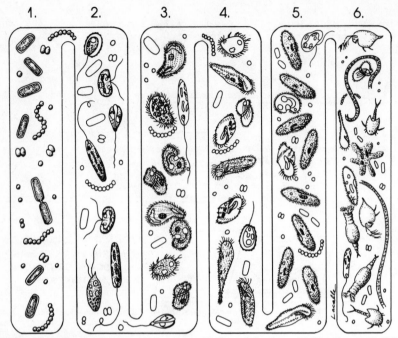

Figure 17–4. Stages of succession in water. (*1*) Bacterial spores. (*2*) Flagellates. (*3*) Colpodans. (*4*) Hypotrichs. (*5*) Parameciums. (*6*) Climax.

as well as catch food. Then draw your food pyramids and food webs showing the relationships between all the creatures. From this project you can learn a lot about the development and interaction of many kinds of life as a succession proceeds.

SUCCESSION IN AN EXPERIMENTAL PLOT

For this study of succession you will need an area of about eleven square feet located in a field. Remove all the plants and animals that are present—at least those visible to the naked eye. Surround the study area with a fence at least 3½ feet high to keep out dogs and other larger animals. A succession will soon begin that may last several years before the area comes back to the way it was originally.

You are going to look at this plot far differently than would the average person who views what is happening with complete lack of interest or comprehension. To you, each plant that begins to grow there and each animal that comes there is a prize to be studied carefully, then plotted on a map of the area and written about in your notebook to the point where you look on it as an individual living thing of great interest. This is what scientists do and this is why they sometimes make great discoveries that other people overlook and that bring our knowledge of the world and its life another leap forward. This is good training, also, for you in observation and understanding.

Different parts of the country have different climate, soils, plants, and animals. These all interact in a way specific to a particular location. This is what makes your local project so interesting, for probably no one else has ever done the exact experiment that you are conducting.

Basically, this is what is likely to happen in your experimental plot. First you may see tiny flat plants called lichens forming on the surfaces of the rocks and some places on the soil. These many-colored plants of simple construction are actually combinations of algae and fungus, totally different plants. One forms the support (lichen fungus); the other (algae lichen) contains chlorophyll, which creates food. Lichens have developed through millions of years the ability to adapt to such extremes as dry hard rock in the deserts or cold icy tundra in the far north. No wonder such tough plants are able to start up on bare ground. Squeezing their extensions or tendrils into the tiniest crack, they begin the process of making soil that will eventually be usable by other plants.

The bare ground of your plot has some soil already, so very soon other small plants, such as red-stemmed filaree, wild pinks, fleabanes, and groundsels which are hardy and need grow only a few inches high to produce flowers, may begin to grow out of the hard soil. Each plant should be named and numbered in your notebook and its exact height measured during the seasons of the growing year—spring, summer, and fall. In fall most of these plants die but spread their seeds for a new crop and drop their leaves and dying bodies to form new soil.

The second year the same basic plants may start up again, but with a few newcomers. By checking your notes from the previous year, you can see that larger plants develop the second year because the good soil has become a little deeper from the death of the previous year's plants. Again, mark each old and new species with a number; locate the numbers on your map. Put the records of heights and rate of growth in your notebook, plus anything else of interest about the plants.

Probably by the third year, you will be getting more grasses and other grassland plants that will grow high enough to crowd and shade out the smaller plants of the earlier years. This whole project takes on more interest from year to year, if you become familiar with the different characteristics of each kind of plant—how it grows, how it protects itself from adverse weather and animal or plant enemies, how it's fertilized, and how seeds are spread (by birds and other animals, by explosive techniques such as release of seeds from their pods, or by the wind).

Meanwhile as the plants grow bigger and taller, more and more animals begin to enter your succession plot. At first there are only small creatures like worms, who are vital in first opening up the soil and aerating it, and various insects, particularly the ants and the grasshoppers. Then come the first mice and shrews, whose digging in the ground and excretion of body wastes enriches the soil. Possibly in the fourth year, moles and gophers will appear in the plot. All these smaller creatures are preyed upon by snakes, hawks, owls, foxes, weasels, and coyotes which may come in from outside but rarely stay very long on such a small plot. Each is a sign of the succession getting near its climax state, especially if it is a natural grassland. Each animal seen during each year should be noted in your notebook, described and illustrated, if possible. Photographs would be particularly important to show the year-by-year changes brought on by succession.

To study your succession plot further, try the following activities:

1. Keep a record of the weather from year to year and day to day so you can see exactly how this affects the growth of populations of different species during different seasons.

2. Get in touch with another naturalist in a different state who is doing the same type of study. Write back and forth to compare your projects and see how succession differs in another region.

3. Build a small observation platform beside your succession plot and place a comfortable seat there from which you can look with binoculars down among the plants and see the insects and other creatures more plainly as they go about their daily lives. Keep notes, interesting notes!

4. Identify your plants and animals by name, both common and scientific. First, use books that describe the plants and animals of your area (see References at the end of this book). Second, find biologists at the nearest colleges, universities, or museums who can help you identify plants and animals from photos or specimens. Usually a pho-

tograph or mounted specimen can be taken to these experts for them to identify. But, you usually need to give them specimens or photos in return for their help. Refer to Chapter 9 for information on how to mount specimens of insects. Mounting specimens of plants is explained in Chapter 23.

18

Burrowing Animals

THERE HAS BEEN increasing exploration of living things under the water using the snorkel or scuba gear, but very little study of creatures underground, under bark, or in other hidden habitats. Yet there are many kinds of life that spend most of their lives out of sight and we need to know about them. Have a good camera ready with a flash because you will want to catch some pictures of these hidden creatures. Also carefully observe the actions of insects, ground squirrels, and other burrowing animals and write them down in your notebook.

TOOLS AND OTHER EQUIPMENT NEEDED

A trowel is needed for shallow digging in the ground, while a pick and shovel are used for more serious digging. A crowbar is handy for turning over large rocks or logs to see what is underneath. And a pry-bar is good for prying up bark. If possible, pry up a whole sheet of bark so you can put it back over what you have uncovered.

You will also need transparent plastic sheets strong enough to prevent an animal from pushing it aside too easily, but resilient enough to be shaped around animal tunnels or nests, if possible.

Transparent plastic tubing is used to make artificial tunnels. You will need different sizes from ½-to-1 inch for insects or shrews, 1½-to-2 inches for moles or mice, 2½ inches for gophers, and 3 inches for ground squirrels.* This tubing can be cut in half with a single-edge sharp razor blade if needed to cap the top of a tunnel instead of completely rounding it out.

Waterproof black paper sheets, such as roofing paper, are for roofing over tunnels or underground nests that have been exposed and to keep out light. Each piece of paper needs to be cut to fit the special project it is being used for.

A flashlight with red plastic cover is used for viewing animals in their tunnels and nests at night. The red light, though making them perfectly visible to humans, is usually not disturbing to most animals like white light would be.

PREPARING OBSERVATION SITES

When preparing underground views, digging, or stripping away bark, you must replace what has been removed by something equivalent so that the animals can be watched underground, underbark, or underwood with the minimum of disturbance to their habits and ecology. Therefore, the plastic tunnels or pieces of plastic sheets formed into tunnels that you place in the ground to imitate underground dirt tunnels must be covered over first with black waterproof paper to keep out the light and then by dirt. This dirt and the black paper can be pulled aside at night and the animals watched through the clear plastic by the use of the red flashlight. It is especially necessary to fix a plastic cover over a nest room that is underground or underwood or underbark so that the nesting habits and the rearing of young can be watched at night. Write notes of all that you see.

You can make artificial tunnels and nest boxes ahead of the time the adult animals are looking for places to hide their young (Figure 18–1). Such a box and tunnel can be made of different sizes: one for mice, another for rats and chipmunks, another for ground squirrels, another

---

*If you can't find any large tubing to buy, you might be able to make large-size tunnels by rolling ⅛- or ¼-inch plastic sheets and securing them with tape.

for skunks and woodchucks. Study the size of each animal before making a box and tunnels for it.

The time for putting an artificial nest and tunnel into a hillside is usually in early spring before the animals are getting ready to have families. The entrance hole should be hidden by a large bush or bushes so that humans or other animals are not likely to see it, but an animal looking for a nest hole would be likely to find it. If the top of the nest box is covered with heavy 5 mil plastic and this covered with black waterproof paper and at least a foot of dirt, it will protect the denizens of the nest from cold. Then later in the spring you can uncover the top of the box at night by lifting out the dirt to uncover the plastic sheet, and with a red flashlight study the habits and actions of the creatures in the nest until they are big enough to leave. Use the utmost quietness and caution in approaching the nest and stay away from the entranceway. Later you can watch the young animals through binoculars when they come out to play or their mother brings food. One way to make your animals completely delighted with their nest hole is to have two artificial entranceways, which would give them an extra one to use for escape if a large snake or other enemy entered one hole. Be sure the second hole is also hidden by bushes.

One other possibility for watching creatures underground is a periscope combined with a penlight that is small enough to insert into a near-surface tunnel of a gopher or mole (Figure 18–2). The periscope can be homemade with a tube and a mirror, placed at a 45-degree angle so it reflects what is seen in the tunnel up to the eye which is above ground. This might have several other uses that you can think up.

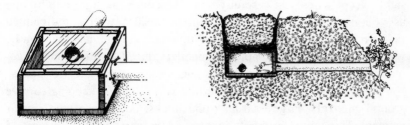

Figure 18–1. Artificial nest box with clear plastic top for observing burrowing animals. Cutaway view (*right*) shows how to bury nest box and tunnel. Leave enough paper or plastic exposed so you can grasp and lift out the dirt.

Figure 18–2. Persicope with small flashlight taped inside for viewing creatures in underground tunnels.

KEEPING BURROWING ANIMALS IN CAPTIVITY

If you wish to study the life of underground, underbark, or wood creatures in captivity, do it only if you can make their homes in captivity as much as possible like their natural habitats. Of course, this can be easily done with insects and other small creatures as already discussed in Chapter 10. But mammals, reptiles, and amphibians that live underground, under bark, or in wood probably can be no larger than a rat for adequate study in natural habitatlike situations without going to too great expense.

A fairly large terrarium would probably work for mice, salamanders, and the smallest snakes and lizards. It should be a long narrow terrarium with glass on both sides and with dirt and rocks along the bottom high enough to give room for tunnels. Most of the tunnels and the nest need to be exposed to your eyes for study on either side of the terrarium. All sides need to be covered with boards or tar paper to the height of the dirt and rocks so that the animals are hidden from sight except when you carefully open the covers at night one by one as you need to, and flash light on the insides with a red-painted or -covered flashlight. Some typical underground animals that can be watched in this way are mole salamanders, meadow mice, moles, gophers, kangaroo rats, blind snakes, gopher snakes, and hog-nosed snakes.

Something larger than a terrarium is needed for keeping captive ground squirrels, large lizards, woodchucks, cottontails, and similar animals. This would probably involve a long narrow cage, at least 15 feet long, with hinged wooden sides covered with dirt. There would be glass on the inside so the wooden sides could be lifted up to allow you to watch the creatures in their tunnels and nests. Probably ground squirrels, which are daylight active animals, could be watched through the sides in the dusk of evening or early morning and you would still not disturb them too much, especially if you sat perfectly still when watching them.

To capture some of these animals you can use the noose described in Chapter 7 or use live traps, which are available at many hardware stores. While lizards, snakes, and large insects are not too bothered by human odors, mammals usually are aware a man has been around and stay away from traps with his smell. I found small mice and gophers were exceptions to this, but ground squirrels, cottontails, and woodchucks would definitely notice such a smell. Therefore, with such animals, you need to boil your traps in water with a strong-smelling plant like sagebrush, mugwort, or honeysuckle. After this, handle the traps with gloves that have been soaked in the same water.

Traps should be set where there are signs of life such as droppings, holes in the ground, or other indications of digging. Baits depend on the animal you are trapping. Carrots work wonders with ground squirrels, gophers, and rabbits. Fresh meat attracts weasels. Remember, weasels can bite ferociously and must be moved from one cage to another through gates and with the utmost care. They should not be handled at all unless and until you are thoroughly trained by an expert.

Before trapping any animal, be sure that it can be legally taken in your state. Check with the state fish and game department about the regulations in your area.

PROJECTS WITH BURROWING ANIMALS

1. Investigate both surface tunnels and deep tunnels of moles in the ground, using an extended viewscope and penlight. Observe how the moles react, if at all, to the light, what you can see them eating in the tunnels, and how they react when two moles meet. Try to distinguish males from females and see if their reactions differ. Record your observations completely in your notebook, with drawings.

2. Try to photograph mole behavior underground if you can manage to get a flash bulb and camera in proper position to take a picture when the mole sets off a trip-wire. (Ask a professional photographer how to set up trip-wires for photography.)

3. Explore a nest of carpenter ants in an old log by removing wood or bark from different parts of a log to expose cavities where ants are

rearing young or the queen is laying eggs. Do this in one place at a time, each time quickly putting a plastic cover that is covered with black tar paper over the exposed cavities and rooms of the ant city. Do this until many parts of the city are exposed and then covered with plastic and paper, both of which have been cut to fit the exposed areas. Come back at night with a red-covered flashlight and take off the tar paper covering from the different excavations or rooms, each time putting the paper back after close examination using the red light so as not to disturb the ants. Ask and answer the following: (a) Are there different-size ants, and do they have different jobs? What are they? (b) How many eggs does the queen lay in an hour? What kind of guards does she have, and what do they do to protect her? (c) What kinds of food do the adult ants eat? What kinds of food do the adult ants bring to the ant larvae for these to eat? If large insects are attacked for food, how do the ants overcome them?

In most ant cities there are various other insects including different, and usually much smaller, species of ants, ant-crickets, ant-beetles, and ant-cockroaches. These other insects may eat the ants' food and sometimes attack and kill ants or larvae. Also, there are insects such as aphids and scale insects that exude a sweet fluid the ants like. The ants treat these like cows and even carry them about on plants to find food for them and guard them from enemies. See how many kinds of these creatures you can find in the nest you are studying. Describe, draw, and photograph them when possible. Observe how the ants act toward these different creatures and how they act in return.

4. Study the nesting habits and behavior of ground squirrels using an artificial nest box. Observe the nest at dawn and dusk and in the nighttime with a red flashlight. What kind of food do the adults bring to the young? What signals pass between adults and young and between the young? What kinds of other creatures inhabit the nest burrows with the ground squirrels and which are beneficial and which harmful? Some scientists think that burrowing owls (found in most of the West in dry areas) go into such burrows and kill and eat the young squirrels, but others think that burrowing owls use the burrows of other animals as hiding or nesting places without doing any harm. See if you can find out who is right.

5. If you find a dying tree or fallen log that shows the work of wood-boring beetles, dig off the bark with a pry, also some of the wood if necessary, to find where the beetles are working. Cover the beetles

or their grubs, whichever is working on the tree, with plastic to hold them in place, and then cover the plastic with black tar paper. Both the plastic and tar paper should be strapped, tied, tarred, or nailed to the dying or dead tree.

Come back at night to observe the beetles and/or their grubs at work, using a red-covered flashlight so you do not disturb them. Identify different species by using insect books or take specimens (alive or dead) to a university entomology department or county extension office for help. Usually each grub, or sometimes the adult beetle, is eating its way along the cambium layer, which is killing the tree. Observe them at their work under red lights at night, and come back another night to record how far they have traveled in their eating paths. Can you estimate how far they will go in a week or month?

6. Study the peculiar creatures you find under dry cow pies or cow chips, as they are called. A partially dried cow pie or chip, especially a large one, may have lots of life inside it and under it. Typical inhabitants include fly grubs, ants, beetles, spiders, and centipedes. Turn over such a chip, and immediately write down all that you see happening on the ground beneath it and within the chip. Then turn it back over in the same place. Come back a day or so later and repeat the process, especially noting any changes. Actually, if you were to examine a cow pie when it is first deposited, and then came back to it every few days for a half year or so, you would see a process of succession in the kinds of animals and even plants you found there, much as happens in the successions discussed in Chapter 17.

Take a large sharp knife and cut the cow chip crosswise into separate layers, trying to find out what is in each layer. You may be amazed at the different things you find. You could take one chip home and put glass under it. Cover it with black tar paper during the day and remove the tar paper at night to examine the life that is there under a red light. Record in your notebook all that you observe and be sure to get the different species identified. There is a story waiting for us to unravel in every cow pie! Let people laugh at you. They don't know the adventure they are missing.

19

Ponds, Streams, and Freshwater Aquariums

IN ALL OUR natural areas, except possibly the rocky seashores, life is never so thick as it is in and around a pond. All kinds of water and shore plants grow along the edge of the pond and in its depths, if it has not been polluted or the life in it killed by too much cold or heat, while millions of creatures swarm in the depths and on the surface. It is a most wonderful place to explore and to learn about the many interrelationships of life.

OBSERVING LIFE IN A POND

To soak yourself in the life of a pond you can first just sit down beside it and watch it, trying to find a place where you can both see in among the shore plants and also have a nearby section of clear water to look down into. You can see zones of plant life, if you look carefully. On the dry shore are land plants that yet love water; then come near-shore plants in shallow water—including arrowheads, pickerel weeds, and cattails—which form another zone of life, with their leaves and flowers often several feet above the water. Beyond these plants and generally in deeper water are the more often submerged plants, such as feathery milfoils (*Myriophylum*), water weeds (*Elodea*), and pond weeds (*Potomogeton*), which form a zone where smaller fishes swim. Deeper still are the plants that float free such as the duckweeds (*Lemna* and *Spirodela*), the bladderworts (*Utricularia*), which use floating bladders, and the hornworts (*Ceratophyllum*), all of which attract ducks and larger fish.

The shore and edge-of-shore plants form a jungle where life is generally the thickest, for the plants not only provide food for the animals, but they also form all kinds of hiding and lurking places for the hunters and the hunted. Above the water on many plants can be found small insects like the aphids, plant lice, or tarnished plant bugs that suck plant juices. On these plant-eating insects feed such predators as lace-wing flies and their larvae and ladybird beetles. In the air above swarm gnats, mosquitoes, and many kinds of flies. Some like the robber fly and the dragonfly are major predators, swift of wing and fierce in attack; but lesser predators, like the more fragile damselflies, abound also. Grebes, ducks, stilts, bitterns and other birds hide among the bulrushes, cattails, and water lilies; some are mainly plant feeders, like most ducks, while others are flesh-eaters, like the herons and bitterns.

The water below has so many forms of life that I can mention only a few. The fanworts, tape grass, and pondweed supply food for the submerged plant grazers, such as mayfly larvae and the larvae of hover flies. Capturing and eating these and other water insects, or even polly-wogs and small fish, are diving beetles, backswimmers, water scorpions, and giant water bugs, as well as dragonfly and damselfly larvae (Figure 19–1).

Living in the open water are bass, sunfish, and minnows, while the pond catfish or bullheads like the areas under the water plants and in the mud better than the open water. All are predators on small fish and insects. The toads and frogs also come into the waters among the plants, especially to lay eggs, which are attached to the underwater stems in jellylike masses. Most salamanders (Figure 19–2) are also lung-breathers when they are adults, though some, like the Sirens, are gill-breathers all their lives, while others, such as the lungless salamanders of the family Plethodontidae, strangely have no lungs in the adult phase, but breathe through pores in their damp skins.

Salamanders, toads, and frogs metamorphose from gill-breathing

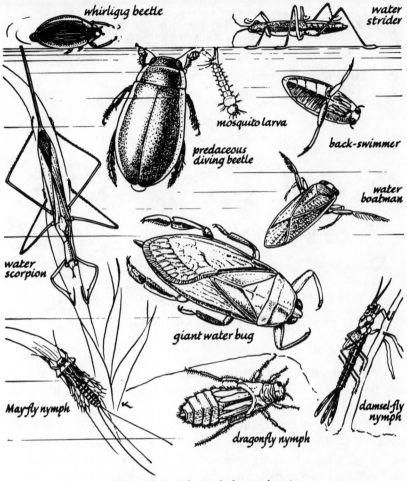

Figure 19–1. A few typical water insects.

larvae, called pollywogs or tadpoles, into adults that are usually lung-breathers (with the exceptions given above), and most travel easily on land as well as in the water. The eggs are usually layed in masses surrounded by a jellylike substance to protect them. The emerging tadpoles derive food from their own tails at first, but soon become vegetarians, feeding on the water plants, until they become big enough to prey on water insects and other small creatures. Some salamanders and some toads (especially the spadefoot toads), hardly see any ex-

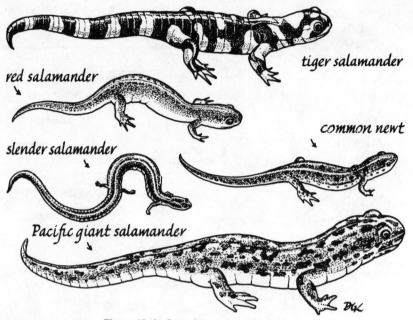

Figure 19–2. Some interesting salamanders.

tensive water at all, the former living in the damp crotches of trees and the latter burrowing in the ground to get away from the summer heat of the arid areas.

There are, of course, an infinite number of other interesting animals, particularly invertebrates other than water insects, that swarm in a pond. Crayfish, cyclops or water fleas, pond leeches, and several kinds of freshwater snails are some of the most obvious ones (Figure 19–6). The crayfish always make me think of comical clowns, as they dash about so fast when disturbed and their eyes and enormous pincers for grabbing prey are so startling. The cyclops water fleas are so named because they have one large eye in the middle of the forehead, and they too dash about in all directions out of fear or as part of their hunting of still smaller creatures. The snails are particularly interesting when they glide along upside down on the bottom side of the surface film, and then drop down suddenly to the bottom when frightened, sliding on a thread of mucus, very much like the threads of a spider. Leeches give you plenty of trouble if you wade in their ponds, for they love to attach themselves to the skin of your legs, piercing it with a rasplike mouth and then sucking the blood. They are not just blood-suckers, however, as they also prey on other worms, tadpoles, snails, and other small animals. Indeed a leech can be a cannibal, a parasite, a scavenger, or a free-living predator. They are far more interesting to study than most people think. You can be thankful that when they eat your blood that one meal lasts them for many days!

Projects in a Pond

1. Snorkeling along, watching the life under the water while moving slowly and carefully so as not to disturb it, can be great fun and highly educational. One thing you can do while snorkeling is to unravel the food chains and food webs of the many underwater animals and plants. Figure 19–4 shows a very simple food chain from a single-celled algae, floating through the water and invisible unless you have magnifying glasses, which is eaten by a paramecium, with its rows of oarlike cilia (also invisible), which is eaten by a rotifer (hardly more than a speck), which is eaten by one of the tiny fish (not shown in the picture),

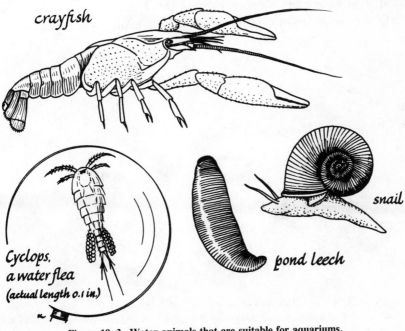

crayfish

Cyclops,
a water flea
(actual length 0.1 in.)

pond leech

snail

Figure 19–3. Water animals that are suitable for aquariums.

which is eaten by a medium-sized fish, which is eaten by a large fish, such as a smallmouth bass, which is captured on a fish line and hook by a man and then fried in a frying pan for his breakfast.

The first thing you do when you come up from snorkeling is to get your notebook and write down exactly who ate whom when you were watching underwater. Of course you are not going to be able to record the invisible part of the food chain until you can get a microscope and actually see the paramecium eating the algae, and so on. There are many other creatures that might be in on the food chain besides those mentioned, such as a heron or kingfisher striking down with a long, sharp bill to grab a fish, or a raccoon grabbing a frog that ate a water bug.

2. You can make a glass-bottomed boat by cutting a square hole in the middle of its bottom to fit the exact size of a box, whose bottom is fitted with a piece of plate glass, cleated and sealed into place with waterproof cement both inside and out. Then, stretched on a foam-rubber pad, you can watch the life of a pond for hours, as you float about on it. But remember that careful notes must be put into your notebook whenever you notice something new or unusual. Food chains and food webs can be drawn to show what you have seen. It would take many months of careful watching, note-taking, and sketching be-

Figure 19–4. A very simple food chain in a pond (not drawn to relative scale). (*1*) Single-celled algae. (*2*) Paramecium. (*3*) Rotifer. (*4*) Bluegill fish. (*5*) Smallmouth bass. (*6*) Human's fishing line.

fore you would begin to see anything like the complete web of life for a whole pond.

3. Take one, two, or three kinds of animals and study their life histories from egg to adult, including courtship, mating, egg-laying, egg and larva protection, and all the young stages of growth. For example, the bullfrog male calls his mate in the spring with his great "jug-o'rum" roar. After mating, the eggs are laid among the pondweed stems near land, formed in masses surrounded by jelly. The young tadpole that emerges from an egg is so small that it has a whole host of enemies— from predaceous worms to water bugs to fish—which it avoids by swimming deep among the stems of water plants or hiding in the mud. The tadpole first feeds on plants like algae, but gradually it becomes a meat-eater and predator, catching water insects and then, when really big, small fish. After it loses its tail and becomes an adult frog, it goes on land to find insects and worms and even mice, but it generally prefers the water at the edge of ponds, living for many years and growing very large if it can avoid enemies like raccoons and herons. Sitting like a king on a big lily pad, it has become one of the principal predators of the pond, able to swallow a fair-sized fish or snake.

THE FRESHWATER AQUARIUM

Figure 19–5 shows how to build an aquarium, one holding at least ten gallons of water. All parts need to be fitted together neatly and sealed carefully with waterproof tape and special waterproof aquarium cement if it is not to leak. It is best to use either plate glass or a strong smooth piece of slate for the bottom, and plate glass sides are preferred too for large aquariums. Smaller aquariums can have heavy window glass in the sides. The wooden frame of your aquarium should be sandpapered smooth and then varnished with at least two good coats of waterproof varnish. Be sure to cut grooves in the wood so that the glass can fit tightly into these grooves; this will give extra strength.

Over the top of the aquarium you will usually need to place a waterproof wire screen or plate-glass cover to keep animals from jumping out. If made of plate glass, the cover must rest on points that allow air to come in under the cover. The cover is taken off whenever you want to feed the animals or clean the aquarium, which should be done at least once a year. All living things should be taken out and placed

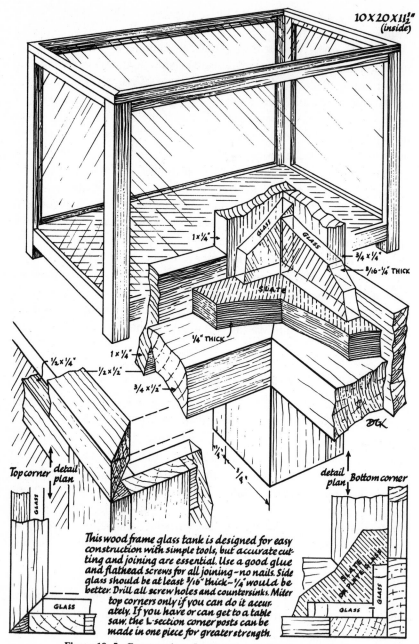

10 X 20 X 11½"
(inside)

1 x ¼"

GLASS

GLASS

¾ x ¼"

³⁄₁₆-¼" THICK

GLASS

¼" THICK

1 x ¼"

½ x ¼"

½ x ½"

¾ x ½"

¼"

¾"

Top corner detail plan

GLASS

GLASS

detail plan Bottom corner

PLATE
OR PLATE GLASS

GLASS

GLASS

This wood frame glass tank is designed for easy
construction with simple tools, but accurate cutting and joining are essential. Use a good glue
and flathead screws for all joining—no nails. Side
glass should be at least ³⁄₁₆" thick—¼" would be
better. Drill all screw holes and countersinks. Miter
top corners only if you can do it accurately. If you have or can get to a table
saw, the L-section corner posts can be
made in one piece for greater strength.

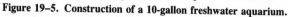

Figure 19–5. Construction of a 10-gallon freshwater aquarium.

temporarily into a big tub or other container so a thorough cleaning can be done.

A ten-gallon aquarium can usually be a balanced aquarium, which means that all the animals and plants in the water are in perfect balance with the animals supplying the needed carbon dioxide for the plants and the plants furnishing the needed oxygen for the animals. Smaller aquariums tend to get out of balance rather easily, and need to have fresh water put in them regularly.

Maintaining an Aquarium

You will need several items to maintain your aquarium properly. A thermometer is necessary for making sure the water does not become too hot or too cold, as both can cause death. A hand bulb with a glass tube attached to it is for sucking small animals out of the tank if you wish to transport them elsewhere, but is also used for helping keep the aquarium clean by taking out the droppings of animals or any small dead animals or plants. A razor blade scraper is used for scraping the glass clean, though this is also done by freshwater snails eating the algae on the glass with the aid of their filelike tongues. A dip net is handy for catching larger animals when you need to examine them or remove them for any reason. Scissors are used to cut up dead parts of plants, which can be removed with the bulb and tube. A pipette is used for taking out water to test its acidity. A dip tube is for removing larger samples of the water and for catching small animals.

A ten-gallon aquarium should contain twenty to twenty-four plants, while a fifteen-gallon aquarium should have thirty-two to thirty-six plants; larger aquariums need proportionately more plants. Refer to aquarium books for information on selecting suitable plants. Fish and other large creatures should not be put in an aquarium until the plants are well established, after about a week or so. If possible fill your aquarium with good pond water, not city water, which may have too many chemicals. If this is not possible, let the city water stand for a few days in large jars so it can be aerated and get rid of the chlorine.

When balanced and kept clean an aquarium is a beautiful thing to see, bringing into your home much of what you could see in a wild pond. Keep it that way. Remember plants are established and healthy in an aquarium when you see them growing runners. Also remember that crayfish may be destructive to plants in an aquarium.

Projects with a Freshwater Aquarium

1. Diving spiders, found in the eastern part of North America, run across the surface of the water catching insects and also dive into the water. When they dive they carry with them air bubbles attached to hairs on their bodies and legs that they use for breathing, much like a diver with a diving bell or with a mask in which air is pumped down pipes from above. If you are very careful, you may be able to reach underwater with a pipette in which there is air, and attach some to the spider because of his sticky web line that usually goes underwater with it. See if this extra air forces the spider to come to the surface again. Some diving or water spiders, an inch or more in length, can catch fish much larger than themselves using their web like a net and then kill them with a poison bite. In the aquarium see how many tricks you see or can make a diving spider do. How fast, for example, can they run over the surface of the water? What happens when they are forced below the surface with a brush? How big a fish can they catch? Perhaps you could even weigh both as described in Chapter 12. See how much larger than the spider the fish is.

2. With the aid of books and the help of biologists at colleges and universities, if necessary, identify all the animals and plants in your aquarium. Put descriptions of them into your notebook. When this is done, you are ready to trace out the complete food web of your aquarium, particularly if you have a fairly good microscope. It will be much easier to unravel the food web in the aquarium than it would be in a pond as everything is close under your eyes. Start with the microscopic animals and plants finding out just who eats whom. Then trace the whole web of life through the entire aquarium so that you can draw it on a large sheet of white paper. Watch out for the parasites as well as the plant-eaters and the flesh-eaters. A leech is a parasite on man and other animals, sucking their blood, but not actually killing them.

3. Divide your aquarium into compartments with a piece of glass as shown in Figure 19–6. Place some little fish on one side of this glass and some larger fish on the other side. If the large fish dash at the little fish to eat them, they will bump their noses on the glass. Time them to see how long it takes for them to learn they cannot catch the little fish. When they have thoroughly learned this, pull the glass out of the aquarium and see what happens. Do the big fish still stop short of where the glass used to be? Do they finally learn that the glass is no longer there? If they learn this, do they then attack the little fish? This is an

experiment in fish intelligence and behavior which is very interesting to find out the answers to.

4. Water striders (Figure 19–1) can be easily studied as they run and jump over the water surface of your aquarium. When a flying insect drops into the water, time how long it takes for the water strider to find it, kill it, and eat it. Try this with other individuals to see who is fastest. Usually the water strider is very expert. Think up many more projects like these with the creatures of your aquarium.

5. In a pond-and-shore terrarium water is in one end of the ter-

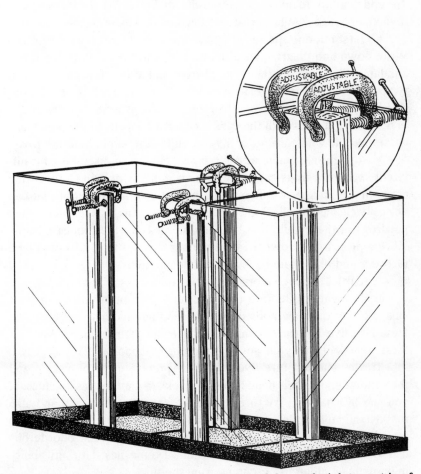

Figure 19–6. Compartmented aquarium. Insert pieces of glass or plastic between strips of wood held in place with clamps.

rarium and land plants, soil, and rocks in the other end. Water boatmen, water striders, toad bugs, backswimmers, water scorpions, diving beetles, damselflies, and dragonflies and their larvae all have different ways of finding food and escaping enemies. Do not overcrowd your terrarium at first, but just have a few of these creatures. Watch them carefully over several days and then draw a diagram that shows their relationships to each other and their methods of escaping from enemies. One by one add new creatures to the terrarium that you bring from the nearest pond. Watch how the newcomers affect and are affected by the other denizens of the pond and its shore. Draw in your notebook the connections to make a web-of-life diagram. What are the most dramatic changes? What creatures become dominant in this habitat?

6. First put one species of frog in your pond-and-shore terrarium. Write down and diagram all of its reactions to the creatures of water and land. Then add another type of frog, and after a few days, a third type. How do the frogs relate to each other? Diagram their relationships. Finally study only one frog to see how it attracts a mate and breeds, what it does with the eggs, and what happens to the pollywogs or larvae. The whole life story may be quite different in different frogs.

You might also have a frog jumping contest and see how far different species of frogs can jump. This is done by drawing a foot-wide circle in the middle of a floor with a paint or other material that can be easily cleaned off the floor. Make concentric circles every foot, then put frogs in the middle one by one and measure their longest leaps. Have a prize for the owner of the winner. Record frog calls on a tape recorder and play them back to get frog reactions.

7. Turtles are even more interesting than frogs as their intelligence is usually greater. (Be sure that it is legal to capture turtles in your state.) Study their methods of getting food and hiding from enemies. How effective is their camouflage in keeping them hidden? Write all these questions and your answers in your notebook.

Turtles may capture flying food by pretending to be asleep and then shooting out their heads on long necks to capture passing flies. If you see this happen, try to estimate the speed of the reflex and also the distance the turtle's head shoots out. Catch some flies in outdoor traps baited with partially decaying meat or something else odoriferous and then let them loose in your terrarium. Do the flies show any ability in dodging or otherwise escaping from the turtles?

You can have a turtle race on the same floor with the painted rings you used for frogs placing about three turtles in the middle. Now see who reaches first the outermost circle and in how many seconds or minutes. Give each turtle a present of a fresh green leaf or a little meat when it reaches the outer circle. See if this can influence the speed with which any particular turtle gets to that outer ring. Owner of the fastest turtle should be given a prize and should give his turtle a special treat.

ANIMALS AND PLANTS IN FRESHWATER STREAMS

Stream life is quite different from pond life, especially if the water is moving fairly fast. Animals have to be able to swim quickly and strongly to go against the current, or they have to find ways to cling to the rocks or plants so they will not be carried off by the current. Most fish in streams of this sort are strong swimmers and can go up and down the stream at their will. Most insects, on the other hand, are clingers, hanging on to rocks and plants so the swift water will not sweep them away.

Caddisflies are an example of this kind of insect, though some caddisflies live also in the quiet water of ponds. Those in streams usually use a sticky substance with which the wormlike larvae attach sticks and/or stones to cover their bodies as protection against enemies. Each larva usually has two hooks at its rear end that it hooks into a place in a rock or plant to hold it safely against the current. Then it puts out filamentous nets that catch floating plants coming down the stream.

Dobsonflies (hellgrammites) and fish flies, on the other hand, have meat-eating larva with strong, sharp jaws to catch smaller insects that come floating down the streams while the larvae cling to the plants in the stream. Dobsonflies are larger and darker than fish flies, some over two inches long. Try dropping insects into a stream so they float by a dobsonfly or fish fly and observe how each catches insects.

Projects in Running Waters of Streams

1. Using a book like *How to Know the Fresh Water Fishes* (see References in back of this book), see how many fish you can identify in a stream. With a stopwatch, time them as they swim up the stream against the current over a fifty-to-hundred-foot course you have mea-

sured along the bank. Which are the fastest? Generally the trout, which tend to be large strong fish, can go up the stream fastest against the current, while the smaller, more dainty fish, like a dace or other minnows, have a harder time of it. Keep records of fish speeds you measure in your notebook. Can you figure how many miles an hour they are going, or how many kilometers an hour?

2. Take a caddisfly larva that is covered with small stones or pieces of wood out of the stream and carefully, with a pair of tweezers, take the covering off of its body without hurting it. Build a dam on one side of the stream so there is a place with quiet water. Place the naked larva in this pool. Watch how it rebuilds a protective cover of sticks or pebbles on its body. Time how long it takes to do this. Compare other caddisfly larva with this one for speed. Watch also how each finds its way back to a place where it can fish the waters with its filmy web nets. How does it prevent itself from being swept away by the stream? You should be able to see how it uses the hooks on the rear end of its body to hold onto rocks or plants.

3. Watch carefully to see how fish catch the larvae of caddisflies, dobsonflies, or fish flies among the rocks and plants along the streams. We know that fish just love to eat these creatures, but how do they find them when they are hidden and how do they get the larva out of its armor? It will take some careful watching to find this out, but it will be interesting. If you can trap a fish in a pool behind a small side dam you have built, maybe you can throw in a caddisfly larva with its armor and see what happens.

20

Tide Pools
and
Saltwater Aquariums

THERE ARE TWO major ways to explore the life of a tide pool of
the sea coast: you can actually go to such a tide pool and watch and
experiment with the life there, and you can build or buy an aquarium
and make an artificial tide pool. However, a marine or saltwater aquarium, as will be explained in more detail later, cannot be used in the
home without considerable expense and expertise; but it can be used
at the shore in a fairly simple way. In either case, the amazing seashore
creatures of a tide pool and the plants they feed upon or live among
are most interesting and wonderful in their appearance and their actions.

EQUIPMENT FOR EXPLORING A TIDE POOL

A large magnifying glass, which magnifies at least six times, can
be used to watch the smaller creatures and plants in the pool. Old
clothes and high rubber boots or tennis shoes should be worn. The
boots are not absolutely necessary, as you can explore the tide pools

in tennis shoes if you are very careful where you step. However, boots give more protection against cold and also various sharp objects that may be found in the pools. Scissors can be used to cut away seaweeds that get in your way of observing animals or to gather seaweed specimens to be dried, preserved, and pressed as specimens.

You also need fine-wire strainers for catching specimens and a bucket to keep them in for temporary observation. Padded forceps are sometimes used to pick up small or dangerous creatures. After a specimen is netted or picked up with forceps, dump it gently into a bucketful of sea water. Tide-pool creatures always have freshly aerated sea water, brought in by the waves and tides, so you cannot leave live creatures in your bucket more than half a day without changing the water or placing them in a saltwater aquarium. Otherwise, return specimens to the tide pool within six hours. Also, do not leave specimens in a bucket that is exposed to the hot sun because they will die if the water gets too warm.

Mirrors can be put down in cracks or corners of the tide pool to give you a better view of these areas and to see how fish and other creatures react when they see their images in a mirror. You might also bring a magnifying mirror, concave in shape, which will make tiny creatures appear bigger and may amaze larger creatures of the pool into thinking a monster of their own species is coming towards them.

Also helpful in observing underwater creatures is a glass-bottom box, which can be pushed below water level and used to shove aside seaweeds that may obstruct your view. This box must be made with waterproof glue so that the glass is completely sealed to the box frame.

A plant press is needed for drying and pressing seaweed specimens. In general, I don't think you should collect any animals to be killed and mounted because there is already so much destruction of seashore life for these purposes. If you do have a good reason to make a scientific collection of marine animals (for example, for a biology class), do not collect rare species. Take only those that are very numerous and make sure that it is legal to collect them.

COLLECTING AND MOUNTING SEAWEEDS

In their way, the seaweeds are almost as interesting, and some are more beautiful than, the tide-pool animals. However, if you are going to collect and mount specimens, do so in such a way that the collection helps increase your knowledge of the sea and its life. Remember that without the seaweeds, many tide-water animals would not be able to survive because the seaweeds supply both food and shelter to many creatures, either directly or indirectly. Also note that certain seaweed species are protected by law in some areas and cannot be removed while they are growing. Check with the proper authorities in your state about this.

Your collection should not only help you identify the seaweeds but also tell a story about the sea and its life. The area along the edge of the sea can be divided into several tide zones. These include the splash zone, where waves splashing at high tide sustain life; the high-tide zone, where the water comes twice a day but only for an hour or so each time; the middle-tide zone, where the water comes for three to five hours twice a day; and the low-tide zone, where the water stays for six to ten hours twice a day. Below the last of the shore zones is the pelagic zone, where the water is continuous.

Observe to which animals of the shore each kind of seaweed furnishes food or hiding places in the midst of its leaves. Some seaweeds are good for humans to eat, too, and this should be noted. Other seaweeds are eaten only by certain animals. (See the books on seashore plants listed in the References.)

Only by studying the plants actually found growing in the tide zones will you come to understand the ecology, habits, and distribution of these species. Gather these plants by cutting loose their holdfasts; place medium- and large-sized types in your bucket with a bit of salt water to keep them damp, and put the smaller, more delicate specimens in pint or quart jars of salt water. Keep the water cool. Very large rockweeds and kelp can be carried in a moist burlap bag.

Collect at least two samples of each kind of species, but do not collect so many you wipe out the plant life on a rocky area. Have some strong, rough paper with you and a heavy grease pencil for writing on it. Assign a number to each plant and make notes about its characteristics when fresh, the kind of rock or other material it was growing on (such as a piling), the exact place of collection (so many yards or miles and direction from the nearest buildings or town), and which tide zone it was growing in.

When you reach home or another place of operations, you had better prepare your specimens for preservation and display using the drying method. The liquid method is usually best done by experts, but the drying method is quite easy. Rock algae and coralline algae (*Lithothamnium*) need to be rinsed in cold fresh water and dried on shaded rocks or boards. The large, coarse rockweeds and kelps should be spread out on clean grass or boards and allowed to dry in the sun until they are just slightly moist. They are then rolled or folded and placed in a large watertight container in a mixture of 10% carbolic acid, 30% alcohol, 30% glycerine, and 30% water. They are left in this mixture until all parts are penetrated.

After this treatment, these large specimens, which are too large to be displayed in a folder or large scrapbook, will remain flexible for a long time and should be placed in plastic boxes from which they can be taken for display when necessary. Each should be identified from books on seaweeds and the name and characteristics of each kept with it on a sheet of heavy paper.

The smaller species, which will constitute the bulk of your collection, can be mounted on drawing paper (11½ by 16½ inches), punched to fit a large ring binder. Be sure to reinforce the holes with rings of sticky cloth. To prepare smaller specimens for mounting, obtain or make a plant press (Figure 23-2). You also need some unbleached muslin sheets, herbarium blotters, or folded newspapers, 11½ by 16½ inches; a large pan, such as a laundry tray; a dissecting needle; a pair of scissors; and a camel's hair brush.

Wash each specimen of seaweed to get off dirt and spread each on a piece of drawing paper that is submerged under water in a pan. Allow the plant to spread into its natural shape, using the brush and the dissecting needle to insure this, if necessary. If a specimen is too thick to work well or look nice, cut off some branches or even slice a branch down the middle, while carefully keeping enough of it to show its characteristic appearance. Arrange the whole specimen to look attractive with the brush and needle. At this point, you cautiously lift each paper with its specimen out of the pan, letting it drain for a half minute or so, and then lay it face up on a blotter. About six to eight layers of dry newspaper or two to three blotters are put on each side of a specimen so arranged. Then all the layers and specimens are placed evenly in a plant press. The plant press is then strapped together tightly, and the specimens (up to 50 or even more) are left to dry in some dry place.

A day later remove the blotters or newspapers that you have put between each of your specimens and replace them with dry layers.

Repeat this daily for five to seven days or until your specimens are completely dry as well as pressed. Next remove all cloths and place your specimens on their sheets in a large ring binder. Most seaweeds have enough natural glue in their stems and leaves to make them stick to the paper; but, wherever this is not so, you can either add some mucilage to the water in the mounting pan at that step or use a white glue to reinforce the mounted specimens, letting the glue dry before placing the mounted specimens in your ring binders. On each specimen page write the common and scientific name of the specimen, as well as details about when and where it was found, particularly noting the tide zone.

All specimens should be arranged in your herbarium and in your ring binders to show them by genera, family, and order. Also arrange them by the tide zone to which each belongs or by other habitat features. Your whole collection will be more meaningful and interesting if you combine the plant specimens with photographs or drawings that show the ecology of the seashore. Arrange the photographs of animals and plants that are found together on the rocks and in the tide pools in your plant book much as they are found in nature. You will learn far more about all the specimens you collect or photograph in this way than by less comprehensive work and create a very beautiful and fascinating display.

PHOTOGRAPHING ANIMALS IN TIDE POOLS

I urge you to carry out your adventures with the animals of the tide pools and the rocks that surround them with the aid of photography and special instruments to help you get better photographs under water, and by snorkeling. Of course, if you want to go deeper into the sea for photography and exploration, you will need to learn scuba diving and buy suitable equipment. This is very expensive, however, and in this book I discuss less expensive techniques. Later when you are ready, you may want to take courses on scuba diving and get the proper equipment. The deep sea is a whole other world.

The reason I prefer photographing animals rather than collecting specimens is that the pressure of the human population on the beaches now is far too great and dangerous to the animal life there to allow for collecting specimens except by trained scientists working for universities or museums and with permits. Plants are different. They grow back far more quickly than do animals; however, rare plants are an exception, and they should be left alone, too.

I suggest that you get a good book on wildlife photography, especially one that discusses methods for underwater photography. Study this very carefully to determine the equipment you will need and how to use it in different situations. Photography can be very exciting and rewarding if you learn to do it right; but, it is very frustrating and disappointing if you use the wrong kind of camera or methods to do the job.

Equipment for Photographing Tide-pool Animals

To make a waterscope (Figure 20–1), fit a glass or plastic viewport into one end of an aluminum or plastic pipe and attach a snorkeling face mask to the other end. Use waterproof glue to make the connections tight. You can glue a screen-door handle on one side for easy carrying. Use the waterscope by placing your face into the snorkel mask and pushing the tube underwater. You will be able to see the tide-pool creatures quite clearly through the waterscope. Also use it to push aside seaweeds and observe the creatures within and underneath.

Another kind of waterscope has a mirror placed at a 45-degree angle inside a waterproof plywood box. One end of the box is left open, and the inside is painted black. By looking through this waterscope, you can see around a corner and observe what you might otherwise not be able to. Both of these waterscopes can be used for photography if artificial light can be focused on the subject.

A snorkel outfit allows you to swim just under the surface of the water, while breathing through a tube to the surface, and see many things in the deeper tide pools. The main thing you have to learn with a snorkel is always to breathe with your mouth, not your nose. It takes a bit of practice, perhaps a couple of hours or more, but is well worth the effort.

A tripod is often necessary to use with your camera to get good sharp close-ups of different species in color. Be sure to rinse the tripod in fresh water after using it in salt water, and dry it carefully to prevent corrosion.

You will be able to take pictures of some creatures in and around the tide pool with a regular camera, especially if it has a close-up attachment. However, to get good pictures of animals found in deep

Figure 20–1. A waterscope for underwater viewing. (*a*) Draw outline of snorkeling face mask on a circular piece of wood cut to fit exactly inside one end of a large pipe. (*b*) Cut out hole to receive mask with a sabre or coping saw, and glue mask inside hole. (*c*) Place piece of wood with attached mask into end of pipe and secure with screws. (*d*) Cut glass to fit other end of tube, and attach to pipe with waterproof glue or caulking compound. (*e*) Attach handle to each side of pipe.

tide pools, you will need an underwater camera. Ask at a good camera shop about adapting your regular camera for underwater photography, as this may be possible. Remember that underwater images are magnified, so that creatures look bigger and closer than they actually are.

Stalking Tide-pool Animals

Some typical tide-pool animals are illustrated in Figure 20–2. Many creatures of the tide pool and, of course, all the plants are either stationary or move very slowly. A starfish, for example, takes several minutes to move a foot; a sea anemone or a limpet is even slower. The way to see how far these creatures move in a certain time is to mark them with bright-colored waterproof paint or a grease pencil, then diagram in your notebook where on a certain rock they are found, and come back a few hours later to see how far they have moved. Conduct this experiment with many different creatures in the tide pools, checking their progress several times during the day. Make a graph, like that shown in Figure 20–3, to display the different rates of travel.

Remember, however, that the limpet, for example, is very much a homebody. It may move away from its home holdfast area at night to hunt and eat tiny algae on the rocks, which it scrapes up with its radula or filelike tonque, but it always comes back to its original location by morning. So if you came to record where it was twice in a twelve-hour period, you might assume that it did not travel any distance at all, and yet be completely wrong. It would be interesting to find out what other animals may pull this same trick. The sea anemone is another very slow mover that might be guilty.

These slow-moving animals are fairly easy to photograph, though some may have to be removed from the rocks. For example, to get a picture of a mussel's whole body, you may have to pry it carefully away from a mussel bed on the rocks. And to photograph the underside of a limpet, you would need to pry it free of a rock with a knife. Be sure to put all specimens like this back carefully exactly where they were found.

The fast-moving animals of the tide pools—fish, crabs, shrimps, lobsters, octopuses, and some worms—will generally move away from you rather rapidly and hide under the seaweed or in crevices in the rocks. These you may have to capture with a net and put into buckets, cages, or a portable aquarium (see later section). Be sure to handle

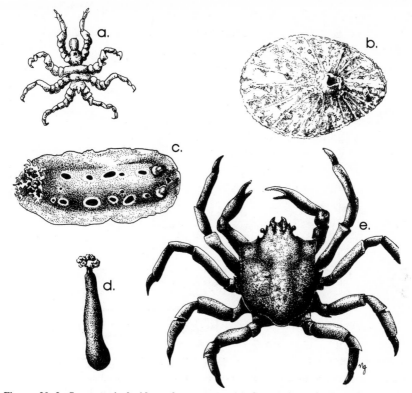

Figure 20–2. Some typical tide-pool creatures. (*a*) Sea spider. (*b*) Keyhole limpet. (*c*) Nudibranch. (*d*) Peanut worm. (*e*) Kelp crab. Remember that the nudibranch must not be moved from its home tide pool.

large crabs (especially spider crabs), lobsters, and octopuses with much respect, probably learning how from an expert before you try yourself. I suggest you first try to photograph all of them in their natural habitats, by waiting patiently and moving very slowly until you can take a good picture.

One way to photograph the fast-moving animals is to have a remote-control cord on your camera, which is mounted on a tripod or placed on the rocks or even underwater, if it is waterproof. Then, from a distance, you can take a picture of some creature when it emerges from its hiding place. Be sure you focus your remote-control camera

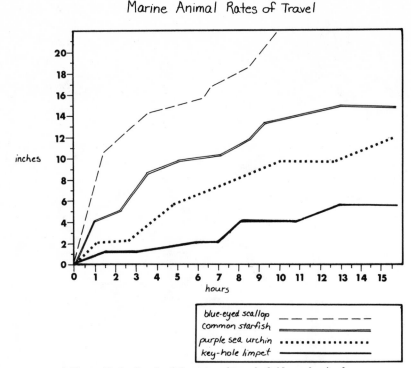

Figure 20–3. Graph of the rates of travel of tide-pool animals.

on the last place where you saw the fish, crab, or other creature you are trying to photo. Then catch it in the picture when it comes into the same place again. This is not easy work. It takes time, patience, and savvy, all a part of growing to be a photographer-naturalist. It is well worth the effort, however, when you get a fine picture in the natural habitat. (Warning: Watch the rising tide and make sure it does not catch you!)

If you are patient, and perhaps lucky, you may observe the tide-pool animals exhibiting different kinds of behavior. Try to photograph examples of some of the following behaviors:

- *Ingestive* attack and flight (one animal trying to catch and eat another).
- *Elimination* of body wastes.
- *Care-giving* (protection and help to the young).
- *Care-soliciting* (seeking or asking for food from parents).

- *Maintenance* (different grooming actions of members of the same or different species).
- *Shelter-seeking* (for example, when a crab hides under a rock or a fish hides in the seaweeds).
- *Exploratory* (for example, when an individual finds itself in an unfamiliar area and cautiously explores it, especially to find hiding places).
- *Sexual* (actions taken during courtship and mating).
- *Agonistic* (dominating behavior and submissive behavior between members of the same or different species).
- *Communicative* (transmission of information from one animal to another).
- *Allelomimetic* (synchronized movements of groups such as schools of fish all moving together).
- *Home range and territorial behavior* (defense by an individual of its territory by action, sound, odor, or other means; males and females of the same species may act differently).
- *Social* (members of the same species acting together to find food).
- *Density-dependent behaviors* (responses to stresses that occur when a species either becomes too numerous or too few to act in normal ways any more).

As noted earlier, the fast-moving creatures in a tide pool tend to dash for cover whenever a human observer comes near. But, if you sit near the pool and are very quiet for a time, gradually this life comes out and may even become used to you and not alarmed if you move very slowly. It is when life is acting normal in the pool and not alarmed that you need to take your photographs, if possible. Be very patient and, in time, your patience will win you good pictures.

USING AN EMPTY FRESHWATER AQUARIUM AT THE SEA

Marine aquariums are very expensive and difficult to maintain, so I do not advise you to try it. Instead, bring an empty aquarium to the sea and place rocks and plants in it to make it look like a tide pool inside. Then place your animals in it, except those large animals like crabs that might be too aggressive. Because some of the animals (starfish and sea urchins) are used to moving with the changing of the tides you need to have ramps up which they can climb to get out of the water for a time. If they do not move back in time they will die of dehydration so they may have to be forcibly moved.

The sea water in the tank will loose water through evaporation and this must be replaced with new sea water for as long as you have your tank in use on the shore. I suggest this not be more than four hours. Be sure to put in a good supply of the seaweed called sea lettuce, as this is a major food supply for some sea creatures. No metal parts of your aquarium should come in contact with the sea water as they will be corroded. Typical creatures that can be put into your aquarium are shown in Figure 20–4.

The aquarium for marine life needs to have a base of clean sand on which you can place rocks to which seaweeds are already attached. Arrange the whole environment so as to look as much as possible like a natural tide pool. Then you can take photographs of the different species of animals in the pool at your leisure.

A little mud mixed with the sand in one part of the bottom may be a good place, if rocks also are near, for the peanut worms of which genera *Phascolosoma* and *Themiste* on the Pacific Coast are examples. The giant sipunclid worm (*Phascolosoma gouldii*) is found along the New England coast burrowing in sandy-mud or sand sometimes under rocks. Sea spiders are not spiders at all, but look like them and are extremely interesting creatures. The flat-bodied sea spider (*Pycnogonum littorale*) is found under stones from Nova Scotia to Long Island Sound. Similar spiderlike creatures are found on the rocks and seaweeds of the Pacific Coast. Still more interesting and far more beautiful are the nudibanches or sea slugs, such as the sea lemon (*Archidoris montereysis*) of the Pacific Coast and the crowned sea slug (*Doto coronata*) found in shallow water from Labrador to New Jersey.

Photographs of all these creatures can be put into your large ring binders with your mounted specimens of seaweeds and other seashore plants. Every picture of an animal should have with it a description of where it is found, in what tide zones and other habitat features such as under rocks, under seaweeds, or on top of mid-tide rocks.

EXPERIMENTS WITH SEASHORE ANIMALS

1. Study the hunting techniques of the common starfishes (*Asterias forbesi* and *Asterias vulgaris* on the Atlantic Coast; *Pisaster ochraceus* on the Pacific Coast). Sometimes these starfish move as invading

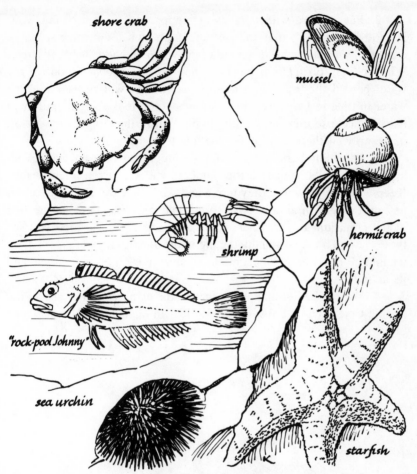

Figure 20–4. Some seashore animals suitable for a marine aquarium.

armies into masses of mussels on the rocks or acorn barnacles to attempt to break open their shells and get inside to eat them. Do the starfish use any special techniques of getting at the massed shells? Are the closely massed shells of the barnacles and mussels a good defense against starfish attack? Which kinds of food do the starfish like most? How do they attack their cousins, the sea urchins? Sea urchins not only have spines to resist attack, but small biting jaws on the outsides of their shells. Watch carefully how they use these defensive weapons to keep the starfish away. How successful are they? Take many photos and notes.

2. Put a board with notches or bumps on it at a slant into your seaside aquarium so that animals can climb on it. See which seashore creatures use this board to get out of the water and how fast they move. Why do they do it? Is it because they are used to being out of the water part of the time? Test them to see if they will go back into the water in time to stay alive; or, if they begin to look too dry, put them back in because they apparently do not realize the danger they are in, but simply sit there waiting for the tide to come.

3. Paint numbers on the different animals in your aquarium with a grease paint or pencil so the numbers will stay even under water. Keep a record of where they move and what they do. Do they exhibit any differences in ability. Also, time their movements from one side of the aquarium to the other. Keep a record of all the food you see them eat and how. Gradually the life in the aquarium will take on more meaning for you as you become familiar with each type of animal and its activities.

4. Watch the hunting techniques of the giant sunflower star of the Pacific Coast which grows up to 3¼ feet in diameter. This voracious

Figure 20–5. A spiny sun star.

and deadly predator is feared by many other creatures. You can watch it only at very lowest tide as it cannot stand the drying out that happens in the higher tide areas. But it is amazing to see a scallop with its beautiful blue-green eyes peering out from under its partly open shell react swiftly when the giant sunflower star approaches. The scallop claps its shells together to force a jet of water out and this propels it off to escape. If the giant sunflower star catches any shellfish, crab, or other such creature, it wraps its many arms around the prey and breaks the shell open with powerful suction, then everts its stomach out from inside its own body to digest its food in a most peculiar way. Keep notes and photos on all its antics.

Almost equally dangerous to other creatures are the 7- to 13-armed purple sun star of the Atlantic Coast from Cape Cod northward and the 8- to 14-armed spiny sun star, which lives as far south as New Jersey (Figure 20–5).

21

Denizens of the Desert Night

THE TRULY HOT deserts such as the Chihuahua Desert, the Mohave Desert, and the large Colorado-Sonora Desert that extends deep into Mexico are hot for most of the year and may be so hot on a summer day that it is almost impossible to do anything but jump in a swimming pool or spend your time in an artificially cooled house. But any one of these deserts, especially during the few days after a rainy period (usually in July-September), can give you one of the most fantastic experiences you have ever imagined at night. That rain, if sufficient, can bring forth an amazing variety of interesting life on a desert night.

There is some danger in that night which adds spice to your exploring it and will frighten away the timid. Actually, the danger is very unlikely to become serious unless you are careless. If you learn the proper rules and follow them, you will probably be as safe at night in one of these deserts as in your own home. But you have to be watchful and be careful or else poisonous snakes, lizards, or scorpions might harm you.

You need to wear a pair of good boots at least three inches higher than your ankles. Wear long jeans or rough pants that drape several inches over the top of the boots and that can be tied so your legs are protected. This gives you considerable protection against bites by a rattlesnake and also protects you from the poisonous coral snake, scorpion, large centipede, and other poisonous creatures. You should stay on established trails most of the time, though short trips off trails are permissible provided you do not get tangled in cholla cactus or other thorny shrubs that can pierce through cloth to your skin.

A powerful flashlight or lantern is a must. The glass should be covered with red plastic so that it gives a red light that does not disturb the night life. Using this red light you can see your way plainly in the desert night and find the fascinating creatures that come out in the dark. You can also see many creatures that are active in the early evening and in the dawn during times when the heat is not unbearable.

Also bring along a folding canvas chair or stool on which to sit while observing the desert denizens (Figure 21–1). This is more comfortable than sitting on the ground and is safer, as you will be above any of the stinging, poisonous creatures that may be about.

CREATURES TO LOOK FOR

Walk slowly along and watch carefully, paying particular attention to the different plants and the area around their bases. Move slowly so you don't disturb the creatures you are looking for and cause them to run away before you can see them.

There are several kinds of scorpions you are likely to catch sight of, particularly in rocky areas or around fallen and decaying trees or logs. The giant hairy hadrurus scorpion (Figure 21–2) looks the most dangerous because of its large size, up to four inches or more, but it is actually much less dangerous than the sculptured centurroides, a slender yellowish scorpion of southern Arizona. This scorpion is so poisonous it can kill children or adults with heart conditions. All scorpions, of course, give painful stings if touched.

Watch the scorpions crawling over the desert floor or up on the plants and rocks. They can move fast if scared or if attacking some insect or worm on which they feed. In the attack, the pincers in front are used to seize the insect. Then the poisonous sting is carried forward swiftly over the head and plunged into the creature under attack. It is

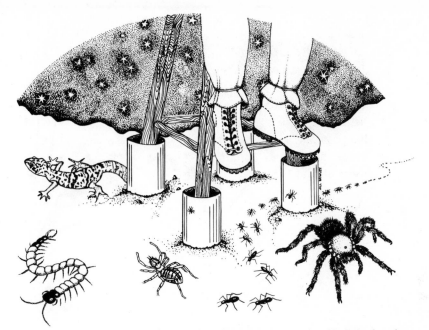

Figure 21–1. A safe observation post for watching desert creatures. *Clockwise from lower left:* **giant centipede** (*Scolopandra heros*)**, banded gecko, army ants, tarantula, sun spider.**

fortunate, indeed, they are not as big as we are. They would be more ferocious attackers than a tiger and just as deadly. But of even more interest is the scorpion's mating dance. The male grabs the female's pincers with his pincers and the two begin a strange and graceful dance, which is different for each species of scorpion. It may be round and round or back and forth and in different directions.

A giant vinegaroon or whip-scorpion of the desert is found under rocks, debris, and logs and in crevices. It looks even more dangerous than the giant hairy scorpion, but really is not. It is not poisonous though it can give a severe bite with its large jaws. It is black all over and has a long whip tail. Much less is known about its habits than about those of the true scorpions.

The sun spider has four or more overlapping front jaws which act like a grinding machine to grind up insects. About two or three inches long, the sun spider looks extremely dangerous. Actually, it is almost completely harmless to humans, as it is not poisonous and travels with

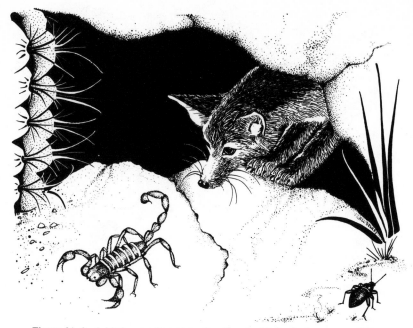

Figure 21–2. A kit fox warily approaches the giant hairy hadrurus scorpion.

such great speed and agility that there is little chance you can touch
it. This extraordinary speed, used to catch all kinds of insects, makes
it so fascinating to watch as it darts about like a streak of lightning.

The even more dangerous-looking hairy tarantula is common in
all deserts, too, though it hides by day in holes in the ground. Four to
five inches long, it moves about slowly, but can jump quickly to seize
insect prey, and has been known to catch and eat mice. At night its
colors merge with the ground; in the dawn and evening it is easier to
see. The female is larger than the male and may kill the male after
mating.

The most dangerous creature to the tarantula is the tarantula hawk
(Figure 21–3), a large blue and yellow wasp about three inches long
which tries to attack and sting the tarantula and immobilize it so a
young wasp grub can be raised on the flesh. The fight between the two
monsters is fierce. The tarantula sometimes wins if it can jump, seize,
and bite the wasp.

Another, very dangerous, desert creature should be mentioned,

Figure 21–3. A tarantula meets its deadly enemy, the giant tarantula hawk wasp.

the giant centipede, *Scolopandra heros,* which grows to eight inches or more long (Figure 21–1). It moves very speedily over the ground with its many legs, the first ones of which are poisonous and act like jaws to seize prey. It hunts all kinds of creatures such as spiders, ants, bugs, and worms, especially under rocks and decaying wood.

On a desert night after a rain, army ants are likely to be on the move looking for animal food. Waves or streams of them move over the desert floor attacking, killing, and eating anything they find. To watch them and at the same time be perfectly safe from any attack on yourself, you can put a chair or stool on the ground with each leg in a can filled with oil so they cannot get up the chair to attack you (Figure 21–1). Watch them closely and see how the army ants round up insects and other creatures they find on the ground or even in some of the plants and then tear them apart to be used for food. If you move fast, you can move the chair to new locations to watch them again and again as they travel over the desert in the night.

Pocket mice and jumping, or kangaroo, rats are often extremely active on nights in the desert after rains, but they can be seen at other times also because they are not so dependent on living animals for food as are the creatures already mentioned. Look for holes in the ground around the base of mesquite trees and bushes; these usually are made by jumping rats or pocket mice who spend much of the day underground. You can make a dummy kangaroo rat suspended on a fishpole with nylon thread (Figure 21–4). Watch how the pocket mice and kangaroo rats react when you jiggle and move the dummy rat.

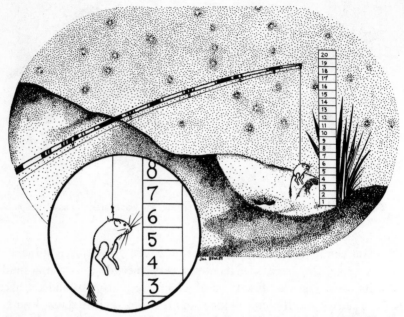

Figure 21–4. A dummy kangaroo rat and marked stick for determining height of jumps.

Even without a dummy, you will probably see plenty of action if you sit quietly on a stool (Figure 21–1). It may be necesary to hide in a blind to get the best observations. Be sure to rub your body and clothes with a strong-smelling plant that will hide your human odor. Especially watch for the interplay of fights and games between the mice and rats caused by either jealousy or playfulness. You could also tell how high they can jump by placing a marked stick in their favorite jumping place or places (Figure 21–4). The marks measured in inches or centimeters should be large enough so you can see them at a distance as you watch closely through binoculars to determine heights of the jumps.

Be ready at all times to watch for the attacks of carnivores on these playing, eating, and fighting mice and rats. Barn owls and great-horned owls are the most likely attackers, but there will also be cacomistles or ringtail cats, bobcats, desert kit foxes, coyotes, and possibly weasels. If you move the dummy rat, it will also attract these carnivores. Observe how each one makes its attack.

Bats are extremely active during these desert nights after rains

Figure 21–5. Kangaroo rats leaping near their burrows.

when all kinds of night insects are flying about. You may even be able to watch large moths using their swirling tactics to escape the bats. It is like an exciting game of hide-and-go-seek, but with life and death in the balance. Taking photos of the bats and their deadly game with a flash can be exciting, but since these creatures move very fast you need a camera with a very fast speed. This is one way to find out which bats you are watching as otherwise it is very hard to tell. If you see a large bat with large spots you are in luck: this is a very rare desert spotted bat. Others more likely to be seen are little brown bats, mastiff bats, big brown bats, pipistrelles, and free-tailed bats.

Each of these bats has a different way of flying and of catching insects. Some fly in straight lines; others dip and twist; still others zig-zag. You can sometimes hear faint squeaks from the bats. These are high-pitched signals, usually too high for human ears to hear, that the bats emit. The signals bounce off the insect bodies in flight and tell the bats how to dive and dip or turn to catch what they are chasing. Some insects, especially large moths, zig-zag so erratically or drop down so suddenly in flight that even the bat sonar is not good enough and the bats miss them. You can have fun trying to figure out which moths and other insects survive a bat attack and how.

Many kinds of snakes are active at night in the desert, especially on a hot night, but usually only a few lizards are active. The lizards you are most likely to see at night are the leaf-toed gecko—a brownish creature with conspicuous toe-pads used in climbing—and the banded gecko, beautifully banded in yellowish-brown, black, and yellow with a white belly. They seem to be the only lizards that make much noise, chirping and squeaking at each other like little birds. They are softer skinned than most lizards and are top-notch climbers, walking on walls and ceilings of houses and climbing trees and rocks in the wild. The banded gecko has movable eyelids, unusual in a lizard. It is often seen on blacktop roads.

All snakes do good in the desert, keeping the balance of life, so you should not kill even the rattlesnakes unless they are near habitations where there are children. Some of the snakes found in the desert are illustrated in Figure 21–6.

The big western diamond rattlesnake, which sometimes looks more peppered and spotted than diamonded, grows up to ninety inches long and is the most dangerous snake you can meet. It is, however, usually very noisy, giving you warning with its rattles, so there is not too much likelihood of stepping on it unless you are very careless. It usually lies in wait, like most rattlesnakes, for its prey, such as rabbits, rats, and mice, to pass close; then it strikes viciously. If the animal is not killed instantly and runs off, the rattlesnake does not have to worry. Heat-sensing pits on its nose tell it exactly where to follow. So it follows the animal to where it is dying or dead, and then swallows it. If you move quietly enough when the rattlesnake is hunting, you can see the whole process, using your red flashlight.

The Arizona coral snake is found primarily in the rocky upland deserts of southern Arizona and northern Mexico. This beautiful snake is fifteen to twenty-one inches long and has red and black bands, separated by narrower rings of white or yellow. It is extremely poisonous, but unlikely to bite you unless actually handled. It warns you it is dangerous by its colors and by hiding its head in its coils, lifting up and waving its tail, and making a popping noise with its vent.

The night snake, twelve to twenty-six inches long, is also poison-

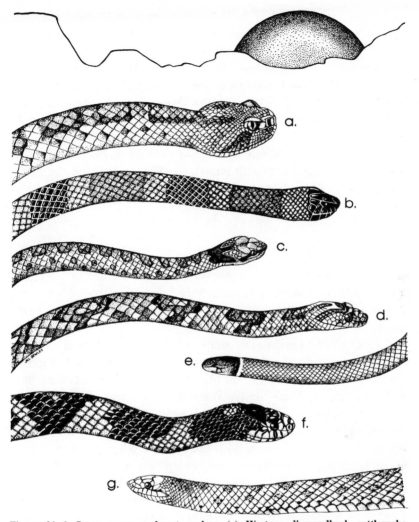

Figure 21–6. Some common desert snakes. (*a*) Western diamondback rattlesnake. (*b*) Arizona coral snake. (*c*) Night snake. (*d*) Sonora lyre snake. (*e*) Western black-headed snake. (*f*) Common king snake. (*g*) Glossy snake.

ous, but only weakly so with teeth at the back of the jaws. It has vertical pupils in its eyes, which indicate that it hunts at night, has a pair of distinctive large dark blotches on the neck, and eats mainly geckos and frogs. It likes dead branches of Joshua trees and other surface litter and is fond of crawling on highways. Its poison is painful, but not really dangerous to humans.

Another cat-eyed snake with vertical pupils is the unusual lyre snake of southern deserts, found usually among rocks where it hides in deep crevices by day. It has a lyre-shaped mark on top of the head and readily climbs trees and steep rocks, looking for small mammals and lizards in the crevices and holes.

Other snakes frequently seen at night are the black-headed snake, the common king snake with dark and white bands, and the glossy snake, faded and spotted in color, but with glossy scales. All are harmless to people, but are good hunters.

SOME EXPERIMENTS WITH DESERT CREATURES

1. Stretch a white sheet between two small trees or posts and shine a bright Coleman lantern or other bright light on it. If it is a warm, muggy night just after a good rain, myriads of insects will come to the sheet.

There will be hundreds of moths of all colors, some of them beautiful Arctiids with yellow and red stripes and other colors, but mostly the sombre Noctuids that seem like part of the dark. Lacewing flies, green eyes gleaming, will dash about on the cloth, while backswimmers and water boatmen, showing that water is near in a small pool, will dash up to the big white light. Here and there you may see the startling emerald beauty of chrysomelid beetles, living gems. On the edges of the light, hairy spiders will creep out, hoping to seize a small moth or bug.

You can do several things to learn more about this dance of the night insects. One is to write down in your notebook all the attacks you see by predators on the light-happy throng—spiders seizing flies, little brown and pipistrelle bats swooping down out of the darkness to grab the moths and devour their fat bodies, a large sun spider dashing like lightning across the sheet to seize a cockroach, and many other hunters and hunted dancing with death. You have to remember that without the flesh-eaters the plant-eaters would destroy the trees, shrubs, and herbs and upset the balance of the habitat.

2. Observe how the different creatures of the night react to the light. Some large moths and big flies seem to want to buzz right into it and die in the heat; some moths indeed go up in smoke when they

touch the hot globe of light. Other moths and flying insects dance around the globe in dizzying circles, but stay clear of the intense heat. Watch what each kind does and write it down in your notebook. The night is full of the mysteries of the why and the how. Each to its kind, each to its way; watch and understand.

3. If you come across a small army of driver ants in long files on the desert floor, get ahead of them and dig a trench with a stick or shovel so their advance will be hindered, making the sides of the trench as steep as possible. Put a couple of stick bridges across the trench to test their intelligence and see what happens when they come. Do they mainly fall into the trench or do their scouts find the bridges and lead the rest to the easy ways across? This is a trick that can be used with other ants on their trails. See if you can find out which ants seem to have the most intelligence.

4. With a stopwatch, time a sun spider when it rushes across the sheet to seize an insect under the light, then try to measure the exact distance and gauge the speed it is making. I know no other creature that runs so fast for its size.

5. Several kinds of snakes like to rest and warm themselves on black pavement in the desert at night. Follow a mile of highway in the dark and see how many snakes you can find. Approach each cautiously and take a flash picture of it with your camera. Identify them later from a good reptile book, and record in your notebook the reactions of each. How many frighten easily? How many coil to strike? A big western diamond rattlesnake would be a thrill to find, but keep plenty clear of it! Be careful always.

6. Place a long plastic transparent tube on the ground and lure or induce some spiders, scorpions, or other ground creatures to enter it. Time them to see how long they take to travel through the tube. You could also make a plastic maze by putting plastic sheets together with glue. Then place meat or live worms as bait at the end of the maze and observe how long it takes these animals to find their way through the maze.

22

Exploring Swamp Life in a Muskrat Nest Blind

THE USUAL WAY of exploring swamp life is to go around in a canoe or other small boat, stopping every so often to sit quietly and use your binoculars to see what you can see. While this may work well, especially if you have a good mosquito repellent and can sit still for a long time, it is not nearly as good as using a "muskrat nest" for a disguise.

PREPARING A MUSKRAT NEST BLIND

The boat can be made with a large inner tube as base as shown in Figure 22–1. The tire tube is filled with air and must be a good one that does not leak. A framework of wire mesh is built over the boat and attached to it so that it forms a kind of dome in which the upper part of your body will be, while the lower part, encased in rubber hip boots and waterproof canvas to your arm pits, is down in the water. In this way, you can walk the boat about in the swamp. If the water is very warm, you can wear old tennis shoes and wear an old pair of pants for protection against leeches.

To the top of the framework dome you attach brush and sticks,

Figure 22–1. Muskrat nest blind for observing swamp life.

either taken from an actual abandoned muskrat nest or simulated to look like one. Inside this disguise place a box or shelf on which you can rest your notebook, binoculars, and any other equipment that will improve your observations. Be sure to make an opening through the sticks where you can look out and be sure to rub your body with the leaves of a strong-smelling plant that will disguise your human smell from the swamp denizens. Now you are ready to walk about in the swamp where the water is sufficiently deep, protected by your hip boots and moving the fake muskrat nest slowly and carefully about to view the wildlife. Be sure to stop moving whenever it disturbs the animals or birds. Watch your step so you don't plunge into a hole.

Another possibility for somebody not wanting to get into the water is to use a canoe with an outrigger (for greater stability) or a flat-bottomed rowboat and disguise this as a muskrat nest under which you sit in a curved framework with field glasses and notebook, observing the wildlife. You could use a sweep oar or paddle to move the boat or canoe when needed.

Be sure to carry mosquito repellent to keep away these pests. There is some slight danger that a poisonous water moccasin in an eastern swamp might try to enter your traveling muskrat nest, but, by merely hitting at it with a long enough stick, paddle, or oar you could drive it away. There is real danger, however, from alligators in some of the larger southern swamps. A large alligator might attack your legs underwater. If you know they inhabit such a swamp, then use the boat or outrigger canoe instead of walking on the bottom of the swamp. Another danger is that some large birds, such as crows or terns, may light on the top of your muskrat nest and proceed to use the place as a toilet! To protect yourself, place a thin metal, wooden, or plastic shield on top of the framework that holds up the muskrat nest.

OBSERVING SWAMP LIFE FROM A MUSKRAT NEST BLIND

Swamps and marshes are wonderful places to watch for all kinds of interesting wildlife, particularly the courting and nesting habits of birds. Figure 22–2 shows some of the birds you are likely to see.

Most grebes breed from the northern states northward into Canada in the spring, but the pied-billed grebe is an exception that breeds in swamps in the southern states. All have fantastic courting dances, some going into rapid-fire gyrations that are most interesting to see. Nests are hidden deep among the reeds and cattails.

Most ducks also breed from the northern states northward in swamps, sloughs, lakes, and marshes, but some, like the wood duck and the mottled or black duck breed in the southern states. Of course almost all ducks pass in migration, and some winter in the southern states. The ducks have less spectacular courting displays than the grebes, but they are still exciting and also, sometimes, very funny (to us).

Most herons, on the other hand, are found mainly in the southern swamps, though the great blue heron, the American egret, the green heron, the black-crowned night heron, and the bittern are also found far to the north. The reddish and snowy egrets keep more to the south, as does the little blue heron and the Louisiana heron. They do a lot of neck stretching and some dancing when courting. To hunt prey, they stalk slowly through the water on their long legs, ready to drive their spearlike bill down for a fish or a frog, or they stand still for long periods, waiting for these creatures to come to them.

Many other beautiful and interesting birds may be seen in the swamp, so keep alert and watch for their courting, nesting, or migrating, as all have their unique niches and unusual habits in nature.

Muskrats are the most likely large mammals to be seen, though the nutria, which, unlike the muskrat, has a round tail and whitish

Figure 22–2. Common marsh birds (*a*) Common egret. (*b*) Great blue heron. (*c*) Black-crowned heron. (*d*) Wood duck. (*e*) American bittern on nest. (*f*) Pied-billed grebe. (*g*) Green-backed heron.

muzzle, is getting very common in many swamps. Both these creatures are expert swimmers and divers, feeding mainly on the water plants. Their main enemy, aside from man, is the mink, who climbs through the underwater doors even into the muskrat nests. If you hear a lot of chattering, growling, and other racket in one of these nests, it is likely to be a mink. Sometimes two or more muskrats will keep a mink out of their nest by putting up a good fight in narrow quarters, but for one alone the mink is usually too fierce a fighter.

Most mammal life is night life in the swamps, with rice rats coming out to play and hunt food at night, and raccoons common all along the swamp edges, but sometimes swimming in the waters. A raccoon can drown a dog that comes after it into deep waters, simply by using its hands to hold the dog's head underwater.

Turtles and snakes are by far the most numerous reptiles in swamps. As these have been discussed in earlier chapters, I will only say here keep your eyes open for poisonous water moccasins (broad heads and narrow necks) and watch for the thrilling courting techniques of some of the turtles, especially the soft-shells and the cooters.

SWAMP PROJECTS

1. Find some insect-eating plants in the swamp (for example, the sundew, pitcher plant, and Venus fly trap) and see how many insects each can eat in a day and how it is done. Keep careful records in your notebook of the kinds of insects these plants eat and of which insects escape from or refuse to enter their traps.

2. Use the fake muskrat nest blind to watch the courtship of birds in spring. Keep notes on all their antics. The grebes, for example, leap high in the air, turn in circles, make outlandish noises, and signal with their wings. See if you can determine what kinds of courtship are most effective. Describe fully in your notes.

3. Make a census of all kinds of birds you find in one acre of swamp land. If possible, do this during the spring, summer, and fall so you can make comparisons between all the seasons.

4. Study the insects in a small area on the edge of a swamp, but, where there is water. Compare the insects here with those found fifty feet inland from the swamp edge. What are the major differences? You should find many more water insects in the swamp. What is the population density per square yard in the swamp or farther inland? Can you determine what causes the large difference?

ADVENTURES WITH PLANTS

23

Protected Wild Garden

A GARDEN OF native wild flowers can be fun to organize and is especially attractive to other people if mapped and explained by signs. Such a garden is also of real value to conservation efforts by saving and protecting rare and beautiful flowers. So many flowers have been destroyed by ruthless and foolish picking and the destruction of their habitats by the spread of cities and roads that some species have been brought to extinction or near extinction. To a true naturalist such a flower is worth far more than its weight in gold. In fact, it is literally beyond value because, once gone, a unique part of life has been destroyed and can never be regained.

OBTAINING A WILD GARDEN

If you own land where a wild garden already exists or could be formed, then you are in luck and can go ahead with all dispatch to proclaim it to your friends and neighbors, your local conservation societies, and your garden club as a protected wild garden, asking for help from those truly interested.

If you do not own suitable land or cannot, at present, obtain some for yourself, this need not stop you. Probably your best plan is to approach your local garden club or conservation society (such as Audubon, the Sierra Club, Friends of the Earth, Wild Native Plant Society, or Nature Conservancy). Learn who will finance the buying of a piece of land near you of the proper quality for a protected wild garden. You can either approach them first and then find some land once you have their support, or explore your neighborhood and find some good land for the purpose that can be purchased. Sometimes a person will donate the land for such a purpose. You can encourage such a gift by suggesting that the protected native-plant garden be named after the donor, and reminding him or her that school children, garden clubs, and many other interested people will enjoy and learn much from it.

Get as much help and advice as you can from any interested garden club or conservation society. Emphasize to them that the garden will not only protect the wild flowers but will also be a sanctuary for animal and bird life of all kinds. You will need, of course, to protect the garden from harmful animals, insects, and weeds. Harmful insects can be fought, especially by encouraging or even bringing in their natural predators. Preying mantids and ladybird beetles, for example, can be bought in quantities for such a purpose.

NECESSARY EQUIPMENT

While a wild garden does not need the same intensive gardening that a cultivated one does, you will need a hoe to remove harmful weeds that may otherwise displace the wild plants. A trowel would be good, too, for the same purpose and for planting new wild seeds. While a water system is not absolutely necessary for a wildflower garden, if you are particularly anxious to save some rare wild plants, you will probably want to give them extra help to stay healthy by fertilizing and watering them. So buckets, a hose, and a wheelbarrow might come in handy.

A book or ring binder is necessary to hold plant specimens that you can show to visitors. The loose-leaf sheets should be 11 by 14½ inches so that plants dried and pressed in a plant press with newspapers can be taped to them (Figure 23–1). The paper must be strong enough to hold the plants without easily bending. Strong paper of this sort can usually be found at stationery stores or you can cut the correct size with scissors from strong wrapping paper.

HOW TO PRESS AND IDENTIFY PLANTS

Figure 23–2 shows a plant press made of two plywood boards about ⅜ inch thick with holes drilled in them to let in air and two straps that can be tightened with buckles. Inside the plant press, you place two corrugated cardboard sheets, then four or five sheets of blotting paper, and several sheets of folded newspaper on each side of the plant specimens. The plants are pressed first between the newspaper sheets and later taped to large white sheets of heavy paper after they have been pressed and dried in the plant press for at least five days. Change the newspaper sheets daily and replace with new dry sheets. This absorbs the moisture from the plants and, at last, gives you perfectly dry plant specimens that will last for many years when properly mounted and covered with a plastic sheet. The mounted specimens, each in a plastic protector, are then placed in a ring binder (Figure 23–3) or on display boards and used to show visitors what your native wild plants look like.

A magnifying glass of at least 10 x power for studying the small inner parts of plants is a great aid in identification. Use a good botanical book and its keys for accurate identification. If you have difficulties, take both a sample of a fresh flower and a mounted dried plant to your nearest university or museum herbarium. A trained botanist often can identify the more common plants at a glance, although rarer species are likely to be more of a challenge. Sometimes, a botanist may be able to identify a plant if you simply phone and describe its details to him or her.

PREPARING A MAP OF YOUR WILD GARDEN

The purpose of your map and the labels that go with it (Figure 23–4) is to help visitors to enjoy and understand your garden. Place the map under plastic on a flat piece of plyboard or masonite, about 24 by 20 inches, and nail the board to 2-by-2-inch posts that are firmly anchored in the ground. Copies of this map could also be made in reduced size,

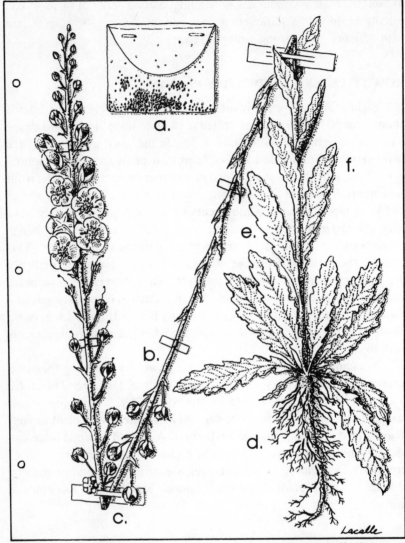

Figure 23–1. Mounting dried plant specimens. (*a*) Seeds in plastic bag. (*b*) Glued-on paper bracket. (*c*) Slotted bracket. (*d*) Back of thick tap roots can be trimmed to allow for even pressing and mounting. (*e*) Lower surface of leaf. (*f*) Upper surface of leaf.

which visitors could buy and then take with them when they wander through the garden.

It is also a good idea to erect signs that visitors must stay on the

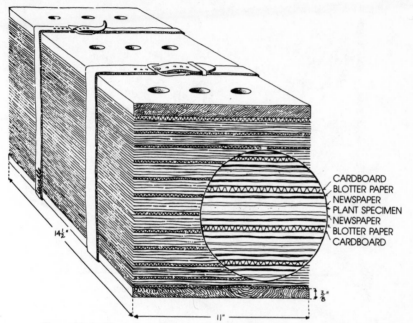

CARDBOARD
BLOTTER PAPER
NEWSPAPER
PLANT SPECIMEN
NEWSPAPER
BLOTTER PAPER
CARDBOARD

14½"

⅜"

11"

Figure 23–2. Plant press. Carrying handle can be attached to top board.

trails and not touch or handle the flowers, only observe or photograph them. Otherwise, your garden could soon be ruined. In fact, when visitors come to your garden, it would be wise to have them gather first at the large map. Explain to them the vital necessity of preserving rather than destroying or picking the flowers. Call their attention to the flowers that are a real rarity before you allow them to wander on the trails.

Mapping the garden should not be too difficult. Whatever the shape of the garden, you need to lay out a grid on it as shown in Figure 23–5. To do this, put a painted stake (orange is suggested) at each corner and measure out the rectangles (say, 30 by 40 inches) with a long tape measure or even a long string that is marked for the size of the rectangles. Sighting along a steel square or a handmade wooden square, with an upright point at the end, will help you keep the rectangles squared. Make each rectangle in the garden by tying a long string around four stakes placed in the corners. Then map that rectangle carefully for the kinds of flowers that are found in it. Of course, you

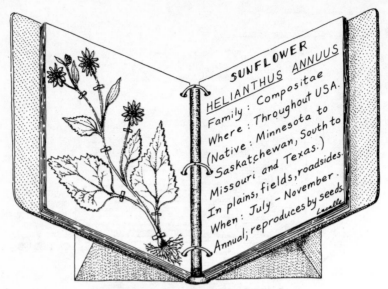

Figure 23–3. Pressed plants in ring binder.

cannot do this until you have identified your flowers, either from botanical books or at the nearest university, college, or museum herbarium.

When such a map is completed, you should be very proud of it. The finished map should look something like the map and its symbols shown in Figure 23–4. Do a neat, accurate job, and periodically update the map as new species are added to the garden.

PHOTOGRAPHING THE FLOWERS

Besides having a mounted collection of the flowers that are likely to appear in the garden each year, it would be very useful and dramatic to also have a large display board on which are placed beautiful color photographs of the different wild flowers in your garden. This would be quite effective in helping your visitors identify and get to know the flowers in the garden. Copies of the photos could even be sold to help defray expenses of keeping up the garden. The photos should be placed on the board so that the different families of flowers are grouped together. Botanical books on the flowers of your state will help you determine what family each flower variety belongs to.

Figure 23–4. Garden map for visitor display. (*a*) Mounted map. (*b*) 1- by 2-inch wood frame. (*c*) ⅝-inch plywood base, waterproofed. (*d*) Face of map covered with rigid plastic sheet.

It's best to use a tripod when photographing flowers in order to minimize camera vibration. Also, a close-up lens is needed to take pictures of the tiny parts of the flower. Close-up photos of plant details are very helpful when identifying plants. A piece of cardboard can be set up as a windbreak when it's breezy.

This whole wild native-plant garden project, difficult as it may look to you at first, can be marvelous training for you in knowing and understanding plants, saving valuable wild species, and having the great satisfaction that you have done something very valuable for other people, too.

COLLECTING WILD FLOWERS FOR YOUR GARDEN

It is not as easy as it seems to successfully transplant wild flowers to your wildflower garden. You often will move a flower you have dug up in a field to your garden only to see it soon die.

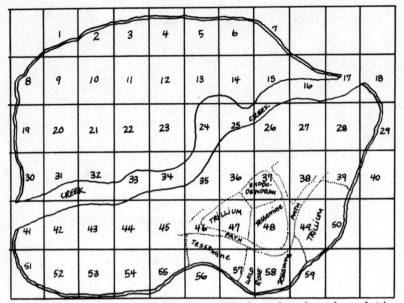

Figure 23–5. Mapping the garden. Lay out a grid in the garden using stakes and strings. Then copy the grid onto a sheet of paper and sketch in the location and shapes of various plant beds.

When transplanting a wild flower, the roots have to be kept in good damp soil in a box when moving it from the fields to your garden. The plant must be put in your garden in a spot that is similar to the habitat from which it came. If you have a friend who is a flower expert, ask for advice about how to transplant different kinds of wild plants. You can, of course, learn from trial and error, seeing which kinds can be replanted successfully. Remember to place flowers taken from woods in a woodslike habitat in your garden; flowers from open fields would need an open area; and plants found near permanent water would need to have a sprinkler nearby.

You can also get flowers from dealers in wild flower and medicinal flower seeds. A list of these people is given in Chapter 24. The owners of these wild flower stores are usually very knowledgeable about the plants they sell and often have mimeographed or printed directions as to how to handle them, where to plant the seeds, what kind of soil to use, how much water they need, and other details.

Remember that each flower you collect, buy, or raise from seeds is unique. There is nothing else exactly like it in the world. Each will have a special way of growing. You should think of them as individuals and carefully study their differences, watching particularly for plants that show extra ability to grow or to adapt to new habitats. Such plants may be real prizes. Describe these differences in your notes. Have a number for each plant in your garden so you can refer to notes about it when you meet it again. Slowly, but surely, you will become a flower expert—at least in a certain field.

PROJECTS WITH YOUR WILD FLOWERS

1. To begin learning how to use botantical keys refer to my book, *The Amateur Naturalist's Handbook* (published by Prentice-Hall), which contains both a simple illustrated key to the very common families of plants and a simple illustrated glossary of botanical terms. By using this key over and over several times to identify common plant families, you can gain expertise that will lead you to more difficult keys.

The next step would be to get from the library *How to Know the Plant Families,* by J. E. Jacques, published by W. C. Brown and Co. This is more complicated and more complete than my book and also has helpful pictures that make the identifying fairly easy.

After you have used these simple keys several times, you will then be ready for the more difficult keys given in large botanical manuals for different states and areas (see References at the end of this book.) Really learning to use one of these keys gives you a magnificent sense of accomplishment.

2. Make a complete drawing of all the inner parts of at least three kinds of flowers of different families, labeling all the parts. Use a razor blade to slice the flower up and down and across, so you see both the horizontal and vertical arrangements of the parts. By doing this, you will increase your knowledge of plants and begin to understand their intricate and varied structures.

3. Learn how to measure the pH of soils, which indicates how alkaline or acidic they are (see the description in Chapter 24). Test different soils—both acidic and alkaline—with three different flowers to see how soil pH affects growth of the different species. Write this

all up in your notebook. Also test sandy, clayey, and dark humus soil to see how these affect the growth of your plants. Notice how a desert-loving plant thrives in sandy soil; whereas, the forest-lover is conditioned to dark humus soil. Keep testing and you will discover other favorable soil-plant combinations.

24

Special Herb Garden

IN THE UNITED States, valuable medicinal herbs and herbs that have other valuable properties (besides being edible) are year by year becoming scarcer. For example, in the Appalachian Mountains, where more of these valuable herbs have been found than anywhere else in America, they have been picked so heavily by both professional and amateur herb gatherers that many, like ginseng and golden root can be found only in the most remote and difficult places to reach. Yet thousands of people still continue to search for these and other plants, many with odd names like truelove, mad-dog skullcap, devil's bones, or lords and ladies.

All of these people need to learn now about conservation and never to pick any plants of these types unless there are plenty of them. However, the danger is that long before such conservation becomes sufficiently widespread many of these valuable plants will completely disappear.

This is why I suggest that not only for your personal enjoyment but also for the sake of conservation, you create a special herb garden of medicinal and other useful plants where you can begin to bring back what is being lost and teach people to respect these plants instead of destroying them by indiscriminate picking. Though I should not give you the idea that immediately you will be able to begin a new business that will provide you with a profitable income, I can state that you will vastly increase your knowledge and interest in some of our most valuable and interesting plants fairly soon. And, in time, it could well develop into a fruitful business, either part- or full-time.

GETTING READY FOR YOUR HERB GARDEN

One of the remarkable things about soil is that no matter how bad it may appear for growing plants, usually, unless it is completely poisoned by the wrong kind of chemicals, you can find ways to improve it and make it support a fruitful garden. Of course, if you can find or buy a place where the soil is already deep and good, you are in luck.

But you can add mulches of leaves and other plant debris to enrich poor soils. Decaying sawdust is also good for your garden soil. You can find sand, sandy loam, and silt along the edges of streams or where old streams once passed and mix these into the garden soil. Be sure, though, you have permission to remove soil if any of these places are on private or state land. Manure from sheep, cattle, chickens, and other livestock is very beneficial in improving soil. Sometimes you can get this for free in return for cleaning up the owner's corrals and fields.

To be both scientific and a good horticulturist you need to know as much as possible about just what kind of soils the different plants you are going to put in your garden will need. Many people who have tried to transplant wild plants from woods or fields to their gardens have been very disappointed when these wild plants did not grow there and soon died. I suggest that you order plants or seed from companies that specialize in wild plants and their seeds. Usually they not only send you the seeds and plants you want, but also tell you what kinds of soils and what kind of climate each kind of plant is adapted to and can develop in.

Since microclimates as well as soils influence which medicinal and other useful plants you can successfully grow in your area, I am including here a list of useful wild herb dealers and a list of books that will help you determine what soils and microclimates in your neighborhood will fit different types of plants. By beginning in this way with the help of dealers who understand the needs of these different plants, you will be able to get some useful plants going in your garden. As you become more experienced, you may eventually be able to collect seeds from wild plants or transplant some from the wild to your garden successfully.

Wild Plant Dealers*

Arthur Ames Allgrove, North Wilmington, MA 01844

Alpenglow Gardens, 13328 King George Highway, North Surrey, British Columbia, Canada

Claude Barr, Smithwick, SD 57782

Central Nursery Company, 2675 Johnson Ave., San Luis Obispo, CA 93401

Crosby Nursery, Charlotte, VT 05445

C. A. Cruikshank, Ltd., 1015 Mt. Pleasant Road, Toronto, Ontario, Canada

Dutch Mountain Nursery, Route 1, Box 167, August, MI 49012

Edmund's Native Plants, 2190 Oak Grove Rd., Walnut Creek, CA 94958

Ferndale Nursery, Asko, MI 49012

Gardenside Nurseries, Shelburne, VT 05345

Hardy's Wildflowers, Route 7, Falls Village, CT 06031

Henderson's Botanic Gardens, Route 6, Greensburg, IN 41240

Kelsey Nursery Service, Highlands, NJ 07782

Lakeview Gardens, 1101 Lohbrunner Road, Victoria, British Columbia, Canada

*Leslie's Wildflower Nursery, 30 Summer St., Methuen, MA 01844

*Lounsberry Gardens, Box 135, Oakford, IL 62673

Eugene Mincemoyer, Route 4, Box 482, Jackson, NJ 08527

Ruth Mooney, Route #1 Box 24, Seligman, MO 65745

Charles H. Mueller, River Road, New Hope, PA 18938

*Orchid Gardens, Route 3, Box 224, Grand Rapids, MI 55744

*Putney Nursery, Route 5, Putney, VT 05345

Robbins Gardens, Ashford, NC 28603

*Clyde Robin, Box 2091, Castro Valley, CA 94546

*Frank H. Rose, 1020 Poplar Street, Missoula, MT 59801

*Saier Seeds, Dimondale, MI 49012

---

*Many of these dealers will send a catalog on request. Those with an asterisk charge for their catalogs.

Savage Gardens, Box 163, Beersheba Springs, TN 37110
Frank M. Sinclair, Route 1, Exeter, NH 03833
Siskiyou Rare Plants, 522 Franquette St., Medford, OR 97501
Sky-Cleft Gardens, Barre, VT 05641
*Sunnybrook Nursery, 9448 Manfield Road, Chesterland, OH 44026
Three Laurels, Marshall, NC 28753
Thurman's Gardens, Route 2, Box 259, Spokane, WA 99207
Vick's Wildgardens, Box 115, Gladwyne, PA 19035
Wild Flower Habitat, Box 251, Beersheba Springs, TN 37305
Wild Garden, The, 8243 N.E. 119th, Kirkland, WA 98033
Wild Life Aquatics, Box 399, Oshkosh, WI 54901
Woodland Acres Nursery, Route 2, Crivitz, WI 54114

Books on Soils and Wild Plants

County Land and Its Uses, by Howard and Suzen Orem. 1975; Naturegraph.

Edible Wild Plants of Eastern North America, by M.L. Fernald. 1949; Harper & Row.

Microclimate, the Biological Environment, by Norman J. Rosenberg. 1974; Wiley, Interscience.

Soil and Soil Fertility, 3rd ed., by Louis M. Thompson and Frederick Troch. 1972; McGraw-Hill.

Soil and Vegetation Systems, by Stephen A. Trudgill. 1977; Oxford University Press.

Soil and Water Conservation Engineering, 2nd ed., by G. O. Schwab et al. 1966; Wiley.

Soil Conditions and Plant Growth, 10th ed., by E. W. Russell. 1974; Longman.

Soil, Humus and Health: An Organic Guide, by W. E. Shewell-Cooper. 1976; David & Charles.

Soil Sampling and Soil Description, by J. M. Hodgson. 1978; Oxford University Press.

Soil Testing and Plant Analysis, by L. M. Walsh and J. D. Beaton. 1973; American Society of Agronomy.

Soils, An Introduction to Soils and Plant Growth, 4th ed., by Roy Donahue et al. 1977; Prentice-Hall.

Soils: Their Nature, Classes, Distribution, Uses & Care, rev. ed., by

J. W. Batten and J. Sullivan Gibson. 1977; University of Alabama
Press.
Using Wayside Plants, by Nelson Coon. 1962; Hearthside Press.
Stalking the Healthful Herbs, by Euell Gibbons. 1966; David McKay Co.
Wild Edible Plants of Western North America, by Donald Kirk; 1970.
Naturegraph. (This has a special index of medicinal and useful
plants.)

TOOLS FOR THE MEDICINAL GARDEN

Besides the usual garden tools, you need a pH tester, a tester for
clay content, and a couple of rain gauges. The pH tester is used to
determine the acidity or alkalinity of your soil. One can be obtained
at any garden store.

Acid soils are good for certain types of plants, while other plants
require alkaline soils. Neutral and alkaline soils are shown by the presence of clover, alfalfa, iris, wild blue flag, and quince. Low acid soils
are shown by the presence of such plants as apples, beans, barley,
buckwheat, cherries, corn, eggplant, endive, gooseberry, grape, kale,
millet, mustard, oats, parsley, parsnip, pea, pepper, rice, rye, soybean,
squash, tomatoes, turnips, vetch, and wheat. High acid soils are preferred by azaleas, berries, butterfly weed, ferns, flax, heath, heather,
hickory, huckleberry, lilies, lupine, magnolia, madrone, manzanita,
marigold, mayflower, moss, mountain laurel, oaks, peanuts, potatoes,
radish, redwoods, spicebush, spruce, and wintergreen.

MAPPING THE HERB GARDEN

You should prepare a map of your garden as described in Chapter
23. On the map, indicate the pH of each plot and the kinds of soil
present (Figure 24–1). Also note any additions of mulch, fertilizer,
sandy loam, or other materials that you make.

It is very important to note which parts of your garden have the
most shade and which the most sun because some plant species need
shade while others need more sunlight to grow well. Probably you will
learn by experience the best locations for different plants. But good
books on the subject, such as those listed earlier, can help you in
selecting the proper location for different species.

Label each species you plant with a letter and number. Use these

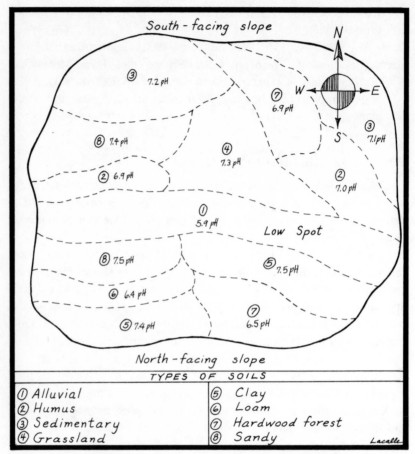

Figure 24–1. Garden map showing soil types and pH.

in your notes and on your map so you know where each can be found. Write about its progress in your notes. You could label vetches as V-1, valerian as V-2, black mustard as M-1, tansy mustard as M-2, and so on, always keeping a complete list to identify all the plants you cultivate. You will want to note all the medicinal and other uses that each plant or its parts may have. For example, you might write the following in your notebook:

Dandelion, *Taraxacum officinale*. Uses: As a tonic, mild laxative,

and diuretic. Habitat: Very widespread wherever there is some moisture and along roadsides.

Big Sagebrush, *Artemisia tridentata.* Uses: Tea made from the
leaves used to treat colds, sore eyes, and as a hair tonic. Habitat: Arid
habitats throughout the West except in low hot deserts.

As you find or learn from others about new uses for your plants
you should write down all details in your notebook. Year by year, the
notebook and your knowledge of these plants will grow more valuable.

As discussed in Chapter 23, identifying plants is difficult for beginners. Yet it becomes an adventure and fun once you know something
about how to do it. See Chapter 23 for suggestions on learning to
identify plants.

Once you have a plant identified, mark your map to show where
it is growing in your garden. Also describe exactly in your notebook
the kind of habitat and the kind of soil in which you are raising the
plant. Remember, you should constantly experiment and consult ap-
propriate books to find better ways to raise the different plants. Gradually, by such research and trial and error, you will learn the best
habitat and soil for each type of plant.

STORING PLANT SPECIMENS AND PARTS

Herbarium mounting of plants has already been explained in Chapter 23.

Plant parts that are to be used for medicinal or other purposes can
be dried and stored in a dry place for long periods provided you protect
them from insects and mold. After the plants have been dried thoroughly in the sun, place them in jars with tight lids. Make sure the jar
top is tight to keep out pests. Some dried plants and their parts are
untouched by pests, if they are kept in a dry place. These could be
kept in string bags, rather than jars. Be sure to label all your jars and
bags with the correct name of the plant they contain, and the uses of
the plant.

POISONOUS PLANTS AND OTHER HAZARDS

It takes a lot of training and experience to become an expert at
distinguishing poisonous and nonpoisonous plants. Beginners must be

very careful not to make mistakes due to ignorance. My wife once cooked for us a very delicious sauce made from *Boletus* mushrooms. She was sure they were *Boletus edulis,* which is a good edible mushroom. Unfortunately, they were *Boletus satanus,* which is deadly poisonous. Our lives were saved by the quick action of a doctor, but it was a good lesson about the importance of being very sure when identifying mushrooms.

You could make a similar mistake with a supposedly medicinal plant that turns out to be the wrong thing or even poisonous until you become expert in identifying species and diagnosing ailments and the plants that cause them. Good books are necessary. You should study several on edible and useful plants, poisonous plants, and herbal remedies (see References). Best of all, of course, is to show your plants to experts and get their advice on how to use them.

PROJECTS WITH MEDICINAL AND OTHER USEFUL PLANTS

1. Find out what medicinal plants can have their leaves or other parts preserved as dry powders for use in herbal medicines. You can find this out from books and also by writing to some of the people who sell herbs and/or their seeds and who may have special knowledge in this field. Start a collection of powdered plants in vials or small jars labeled with scientific and common names and giving information on any curative or other important properties.

Be very careful that all of your information on these plants is correct. A small-scale test should be made before ingesting a larger amount of any plant. A test can be made by taking a very small bit of the dried powder of a plant and putting it into hot water for a tea or mixed with yogurt as a paste. A small taste like this is very unlikely to do you harm, but does give you an inkling as to the character of each herb. Write down in your notes what the taste of each is like, such as bitter, very bitter, or mildly sweet. Bitter or very bitter-tasting plants should probably be left strictly alone. But good taste is not always proof of good quality as shown by my experience with *Boletus satanus.*

2. Find a plant that has definitely proved itself good for some ailment like a stomachache or cough and see if you can improve it by mixing with another plant that is supposed to have the same qualities. Be very careful to taste such mixtures only in very small quantities.

Watch carefully for twenty-four hours or more for delayed reactions before doing any more experimenting.

3. Make a chart of mounted specimens of the poisonous plants of your neighborhood using either good sharp color photos or actual mounted specimens, or both. This chart will help you and all your friends recognize readily those plants that are dangerous.

There are several good books listed in the References that can help you identify your local poisonous plants. Also read a good book on mushrooms so you can recognize poisonous mushrooms, because some mushrooms of the deadly *Amanita* genus are so dangerous that they should not even be touched for fear you might put your fingers to your mouth and poison yourself.

References

Amphibians and Reptiles
Brown, Vinson. *Reptiles and Amphibians of the West*. Happy Camp, Calif.: Naturegraph Publishers, 1974.
———. *Sea Mammals and Reptiles of the Pacific Coast*. New York: Macmillan, 1976.
Cochran, Doris, and Colman Coin. *The New Field Book of Reptiles and Amphibians*. New York: G. P. Putnam's Sons, 1970.
Conant, Roger. *A Field Guide to Reptiles and Amphibians of Eastern and Central North America*. 2nd ed. Boston: Houghton Mifflin, 1975.
Frye, Frederick. *Husbandry, Medicine and Surgery in Captive Reptiles*. Bonner Spring, Kansas: Veterinary Medicine Publishers, 1973.
King, F. Wayne, and John Bayler. *The Audubon Society Field Guide to North American Amphibians and Reptiles*. New York: Alfred A. Knopf, 1979.
Smith, Hobart M. *Amphibians of North America*. Racine, Wis.: Western Publishers, 1978.
Stebbins, Robert C. *A Field Guide to Western Reptiles and Amphibians*. Boston: Houghton Mifflin, 1966.

Animal Behavior
Caras, Roger. *The Private Lives of Animals*. New York: Grosset, 1974.
Frings, Hubert, and Mabel Frings. *Animal Communication*. 2nd ed. Norman, Okla.: University of Oklahoma Press, 1977.

Groos, Karl. *Play of Animals.* New York: Arno, 1976.

Hahn, Emily. *Look Who's Talking! New Discoveries in Animal Communication.* New York: Crowell, 1978.

Hammond, A. E. *How Animals Solve Their Problems.* Carlton, 1981.

Hediger, H. *Psychology & Behavior of Animals in Zoos and Circuses,* New York: Dover, 1969.

Lorenz, Konrad Z. *King Solomon's Ring.* New York: Harper & Row, 1979.

Wallace, Robert A. *Ecology and Evolution in Animal Behavior.* 2nd ed., Salt Lake City: Goodyear Publishing Co., 1979.

Winter, Ruth. *Scent Talk Among Animals.* Philadelphia: Lippincott, 1977.

Birds

Bent, Arthur C. *Life Histories of North American Birds* (a series of many volumes) New York: Peter Smith and Dover. Excellent for detailed biographies of the birds.

Brown, Vinson, et al. *Handbook of California Birds.* 3rd ed. Happy Camp, Calif.: Naturegraph Publishers, 1978.

———. *Backyard Wild Birds of California and the Pacific Northwest.* Neptune City, N.J.: TFH Publications, 1965.

———. *Backyard Wild Birds of the East and Midwest.* Neptune City, N.J.: TFH Publications, 1971.

Bull, John, and John Farrand. *The Audubon Society Guide to North American Birds, Eastern Region,* New York: Alfred A. Knopf, 1977.

Forbush, Edward H. *Natural History of American Birds of Eastern and Central North America.* Boston: Houghton Mifflin, 1955.

Peterson, Roger T. *A Field Guide to the Birds of Eastern and Central North America.* 4th ed. Boston: Houghton Mifflin, 1980.

———. *Field Guide to the Birds of Western North America.* Boston: Houghton Mifflin, 1972.

Care of Animals in Captivity

Brown, Vinson. *How to Make a Miniature Zoo.* Happy Camp, Calif.: Naturegraph Publishers, 1967.

Frye, Frederick. *Husbandry, Medicine and Surgery in Captive Reptiles.* Bonner Spring, Kansas: Veterinary Medicine Publishers, 1973.

Snediger, Robert. *Our Small Native Animals, Their Habits and Care.* New York: Dover, 1973.

Freshwater Life

Klots, Elsie B. *The New Field Book of Freshwater Life.* New York: Putnam's & Sons, 1966.

Maitland, Peter. *Biology of Fresh Waters.* New York: Halsted Press, 1978.

Mellanhy, Helen. *Animal Life of Fresh Water.* 6th ed. New York: Halsted Press, 1975.

Prescott, G.W. *How to Know the Aquatic Plants.* Dubuque, Iowa: Wm. C. Brown, 1980.

Insects

Arnett, Ross H., Jr. *How to Know the Beetles.* 2nd ed. Dubuque, Iowa: Wm. C. Brown, 1980.

Borror, Donald J., and Richard E. White. *Field Guide to the Insects of America North of Mexico.* Boston: Houghton Mifflin, 1970.

Butler, H.F. *World of the Honey Bee.* New York: Taplinger, 1975.

Chu, H.F. *How to Know the Immature Insects.* Dubuque, Iowa: Wm. C. Brown, 1949.

Dempert, Klaus. *The Social Biology of Ants.* Pitman Publications, 1981.

Ehrlich, Paul R., and Anne Ehrlich. *How to Know the Butterflies.* Dubuque, Iowa: Wm. C. Brown, 1961.

Evans, Howard E., and Mary Eberhard. *The Wasps.* Ann Arbor: University of Michigan Press, 1970.

Ferris, Clifford D., and F. Martin Brown, eds. *Butterflies of the Rocky Mountain States.* Norman, Okla.: University of Oklahoma Press, 1981.

Headstrom, Richard. *The Beetles of America.* New ed. Cranbury, N.J.: A.S. Barnes, 1977.

Helfner, Jacques. *How to Know the Grasshoppers, Cockroaches, Termites, etc.* Dubuque, Iowa: Wm. C. Brown, 1964.

Holland, W.J. *The Moth Book.* Rev. ed. Edited by A.E. Brower, New York: Dover, 1968.

House, P.E. *Termites: A Study in Social Behavior.* Atlantic Highlands, N.J.: Humanities Press, 1970.

Howe, William H. *The Butterflies of North America.* New York: Doubleday, 1976.

Klots, Alexander B. *A Field Guide to the Butterflies of North America, East of the Great Plains.* Boston: Houghton Mifflin, 1977.

Lemkuhl, Dennis M. *How to Know the Aquatic Insects.* Dubuque, Iowa: Wm. C. Brown, 1979.

Matthews, Robert, and Janice Matthews. *Insect Behavior.* New York: John Wiley & Sons, 1978.

Milne, Lorus, and Margery Milne. *The Audubon Society Field Guide to North American Insects and Spiders.* New York: Alfred A. Knopf, 1980.

Oster, George S., and Edward O. Wilson. *Caste and Ecology in the Social Insects.* Princeton, N.J.: Princeton University Press, 1978.

Slater, James A., and Richard Baranowski. *How to Know the True Bugs.* Dubuque, Iowa: Wm. C. Brown, 1978.

Spozynska, Joy O. *The World of the Wasp.* New York: Crane-Russak, 1975.

Swan, Lester, and Charles S. Papp. *The Common Insects of North America.* New York: Harper & Row, 1972.

Tyler, Hamilton A. *Swallowtail Butterflies of North America.* Happy Camp Calif.: Naturegraph Publishers, 1975.

Villiard, Paul. *Moths and How to Rear Them.* New York: Dover, 1975.

Wheeler, William M. *Ants: Their Structure, Development and Behavior.* Rev. ed. New York: Columbia University Press, 1960.

Wilson, Edward O. *The Insect Societies.* Cambridge, Mass.: Harvard University Press, 1974.

References

General Nature Study

Adams, Richard. *Nature Through the Seasons*. New York: Simon & Schuster, 1975.

Bellamy, John, and John Sparks. *Forces of Life*. New York: Crown, 1978.

Brown, Vinson, *The Amateur Naturalist's Handbook*. Rev. ed. Englewood Cliffs, N.J.: Prentice-Hall, 1980.

————. *Reading the Outdoors in the Dark*. Harisburg, Penn.: Stackpole, 1981.

Burton, John, and John Sparks. *Worlds Apart, Nature in Cities and Islands*. New York: Doubleday, 1976.

Copeland, Herbert F. *Classification of Lower Organisms*. Palo Alto: Pacific Books, 1956.

Hillcourt, William. *New Field Book of Nature Activities and Hobbies*. Rev. ed. New York: G. P. Putnam's Sons, 1978.

Karstad, Aleta. *Wild Habitats*. New York: Charles Scribner's Sons, 1979.

Kilham, Lawrence. *A Naturalist's Field Guide*. Harrisburg, Penn.: Stackpole, 1981.

Palmer, E. Lawrence, and H. Seymour Fowler. *Fieldbook of Natural History*. 2nd ed. New York: McGraw-Hill, 1975.

Roth, Charles. *The Wildlife Observer's Handbook*. Boston: Houghton Mifflin, 1982.

Sanderson, Isabella, and W.D. Sanderson. *Dictionary of Biolgical Terms*. 8th ed. New York: Van Nostrand Reinhold, 1963.

Mammals

Booth, Ernest S. *How to Know the Mammals*. 3rd ed. Dubuque, Iowa: Wm. C. Brown, 1971.

Brown, Vinson. *Sea Mammals and Reptiles of the Pacific Coast*. New York: Macmillan, 1976.

Burt, William H. *A Field Guide to the Mammals*. 3rd ed. Boston: Houghton Mifflin, 1976.

Hall, E. Raymond. *Mammals of North America*. 2nd ed. New York: John Wiley & Sons, 1981.

Whitaker, John O., Jr. *Audubon Field Guide to the Mammals of North America*. New York: Alfred A. Knopf, 1980.

Marine Life

Abbot, Isabella, and E. Yale Dawson. *How to Know the Seaweeds*. 2nd ed. Dubuque, Iowa: Wm. C. Brown, 1978.

Burton, Robert. *The Seashore*. New York: Putnam's Sons, 1977. Atlantic Coast.

Gossner, Kenneth L. *A Field Guide to the Atlantic Seashore from the Bay of Fundy to Cape Hatteras*. Boston: Houghton Mifflin, 1979.

Guberlet, Muriel L. *Animals of the Seashore*. 4th ed. Portland, Ore.: Binfords and Morts, 1978. Pacific Coast.

Hedgpeth, Joel. *Common Seashore Life of Southern California*. Happy Camp, Calif.: Naturegraph Publishers, 1961.

McLachlan, Dan H. and Jack Ayres. *Fieldbook of Pacific Northwest Sea Creatures*. Happy Camp, Calif.: Naturegraph Publishers, 1979.

Meinkoth, Norman A. *The Audubon Society Field Guide to North American Seashore Creatures*. New York: Alfred A. Knopf, 1981.

Ricketts, Edward F., and Jack Calvin. *Between Pacific Tides*. 4th ed. Stanford, Calif.: Stanford University Press, 1968.

Smith, Lyncwood. *Living Shores of the Pacific Northwest*. Seattle: Pacific Search Press, 1976.

Microscopic Life

Cairns, John, Jr. *Aquatic Microbial Communities*. New Canaan, Conn.: Garland Publishing, 1977.

Carona, Philip. *The Microscope and How to Use It*. Houston: Gulf Publishing, 1970.

Headstrom, Richard, *Adventures with a Hand Lens*. New York: Dover, 1976.

Ishikawa, T. *Growth and Differentiation in Microorganisms*. Baltimore: University Park Press, 1977.

Jahn, Theodore, and Francis Kahn, *How to Know the Protozoa*. 2nd ed. Dubuque, Iowa: Wm. C. Brown, 1979.

Johnson, Gaylor, and Maurice Bluefield. *Hunting with the Microscope*. Rev. ed. New York: Arco, 1974.

Stanier, R., and H. Douderoff. *The Microbial World*. 4th ed. Englewood Cliffs, N.J.: Prentice-Hall, 1976.

Plants

Abrams, Leroy. *Illustrated Flora of the Pacific States*. 4. vols. Stanford, Calif.: Stanford University Press, 1960.

Bland, John. *Forests of Lilliput: The Realm of Mosses and Lichens*. Englewood Cliffs, N.J.: Prentice-Hall, 1971.

Britton, Nathaniel, and Addison Brown. *Illustrated Flora of the Northern United States, Canada, and the British Possessions*. 3 vols. New York: Dover, 1970.

Cobb, Houghton. *A Field Guide to the Ferns and Their Related Families*. Boston: Houghton Mifflin, 1977.

Cronquist, Arthur, et al. *Intermountain Flora: Vascular Plants of the Pacific Northwest*. Riverside, N.J.: Hafner Press, 1972.

Nelson, R. *Handbook of Rocky Mountain Plants*. 2nd rev. ed. Kingman, Arizona: King Publishers, 1970.

Gray, Asa. *Manual of Botany*. 8th ed. New York: Van Nostrand Rheinhold, 1950. Covers most of the eastern United States.

Grout, A.J. *Mosses with Hand Lens and Microscopes*. J. Johnson Publishers, 1972.

Harrington, H.D. *How to Identify Grasses and Grass-like Plants*. Chicago: Swallow Press, 1977.

Kearney, Thomas H. *Arizona Flora*. 2nd rev. ed. Berkeley, Calif.: University of California Press, 1960.

Long, Robert W., and Olga Lakela. *A Flora of Tropical Florida*. Miami, Fla.: Banyan Books, 1976.

Munz, Philip, and David Keck. *A California Flora and Supplement*. Berkeley, Calif.: University of California Press, 1973.

Puhl, Richard W. *How to Know the Grasses*. 3rd ed. Dubuque, Iowa: Wm. C. Brown, 1978.

Rydberg, Per. *Flora of the Prairies and Plains of North America*. New York: Dover, 1971.

Tidestrom, I. *Flora of Utah and Nevada*. Monticello, N.Y.: Lubrecht & Cramer, 1969.

Wooton, E.O., and P.C. Standley. *Flora of New Mexico*. Monticello, N.Y.: Lubrecht & Cramer, 1971.

Spiders

Comstock, John H. *Spider Book,* Rev. ed. Edited by W. J. Gertsch. Ithaca, N.Y.: Comstock Publishing, 1948.

Headstrom, Richard. *Spiders of the United States*. Cranbury, N.J.: A. S. Barnes, 1972.

Kaston, B. J. *How to Know the Spiders*. 3rd ed. Dubuque, Iowa: Wm. C. Brown, 1978.

Levi, Herbert, and Lorna Levi. *Spiders and Their Kin*. Racine, Wis.: Western Publishing, 1976.

Witt, Peter N., and Jerome S. Rovner. *Communication, Mechanisms & Ecological Significance*. Princeton, N.J.: Princeton University Press, 1982.

Index

Algae, 157, 159, 161, 177
Amoebas, 159
Ant beetles, 170
Ant cockroaches, 170
Ant crickets, 170
Antlions, 109–13
    feats of strength, 110
    placed in cage-box, 111
    testing antlion throws,
      112–13
Ants, 16, 99–107, 207, 213
    army, 106–7, 207, 213
    behavior of, 103–7
    carpenter, 103
    driver, 106–7, 213
    experiments with, 105–7
    fire, 99
    fungus, 106
    harvester, 105–6
    honey, 105
    leaf-cutting, 106
    mound-building, 103
    nests
      artificial, 100–2
      digging and capturing,
        102–3
      queen, 100, 102
Aphids, 170
Aquarium, fresh-water, 179–81.
    See also Pond life
    equipment for, 181
    keeping, 179–80
Aquarium projects, freshwater,
    182–93
    diving spiders, 182
    fish experiments, 192–93
    food webs, 192
    water striders, 183
Aquarium projects, saltwater,
    197–200
    nudibranches, 198
    sea slugs, 198
    sea spiders, 198
    sea worms, 198–99
Aquarium, saltwater. *See* Tide
    pools

Back swimmers, 212
Bacteria, 157–58
Bear, 20
Beetles, 68, 84, 170–71
    bombardier, 68
    chrysomelid, 212
    darkling, 68
    ladybird, 224
Biological supply houses, 189
Bird nests, 44
Bird(s)
    attracting, 30–31
    behavior, observing, 45–56
    cafeteria, 32
    crows, 217
    feeding, 31–35, 46, 49, 50
    flickers, 46
    houses, 38–44
    kingbirds, 37
    pools, 29–31
    protecting, 36, 41, 44
    purple martin, 42–44
    roosting box for, 37
    starlings, 46
    terns, 217
    trolley feeder for, 32
    water heaters for, 30–31
Blinds, 13
    equipment for, 216
    muskrat nest, 215–17
Boat, glass-bottomed, 178
Boatswain's chair, 147–49
Bobcat. *See* Wildcat
Burrowing animals, 165–71
    ants, 169–71
    artificial nests and tunnels,
        166, 168
    beetles, 170–71
    blind snakes, 168
    chipmunks, 165
    fly grubs, 171
    gophers, 168
    gopher snakes, 168
    ground squirrels, 165–66, 168,
        170
    hog-nosed snake, 168

    kangaroo rats, 168
    meadow mice, 168
    moles, 168
    mole salamanders, 168
    periscope for viewing, 167
    preparing observation sites
        for, 166
    rabbits, 168
    rats, 166
    skunks, 167
    spiders, 171
    terrariums for, 169
    tools for studying, 165–66
    weasels, 169
    woodchucks, 167
Butterflies, 68, 86, 98
    monarch caterpillar, 68
    sugar baits for, 86
    western parsley swallowtail,
        98

Cages, habitat, 92
Cockroach, 212
Colpodans, 158
Copepods, 159
Cowparsnip, 171
Coyote, 20, 162, 208
Crows, 24, 51
    talking, 51–54

Desert denizens, 204–12
    army ants, 104–7, 207
    bats, 208–9
    bobcats, 208
    coyotes, 208
    desert kit foxes, 208
    experiments with attracting
        insects, 212
    geckos, 210
    giant centipede, 207
    kangaroo rats, 217
    mice, 206
    moths, 209
    owls, 208

pocket mice, 207
rattlesnakes, 210
ringtail cats, 208
scorpions, 204–5
snakes, 210–12
sun spider, 205–6, 212, 213
tarantula, 206
tarantula hawk, 206
weasels, 208
Dummies, animal and bird, 19–20,
50–51, 53

Falcon, prairie, 69
Filaree, red-stemmed, 161
Flagellates, 157
Fleabanes, 161
Food chains, 95, 156
Food pyramid, 157
Food web, 156
Foxes, 20, 77, 162
kit, 208
tracks, 146
Freshwater streams
animals and plants of, 185–87
projects for, 185–86
Frogs, 153, 174–75
Fungus, 161

Garden, native wild
collecting wildflowers for,
229–31
equipment for, 224–25
finding and developing, 223–24
mapping, 225–26
projects with wildflowers,
231–32
Gophers, 162
Grass blade squeaker, 24
Grasshoppers, 162
Groundsels, 161

Habitats, temperature and
humidity of, 91

Hawks
Cooper's, 36, 44
marsh, 24
prairie falcon, 69
red-tailed, 23
sharp-shinned, 36
sparrow, 36
Swainson's, 24
white-tailed kite, 69
Herb garden, 233–41
mapping, 237–38
Ph testing, 237
poisonous plants, 239–40
preparing, 234–36
projects with, 240–41
storing plant specimens, 239
Hiding from animals, 25
Hummingbirds, feeding, 35
Hypotrichs, 159

Insects, 81–118
antlions, 109
ants, 99–107, 110
baits, 86
bristle-tails, 98
crash nets, 82
cricket, 98
identification, 86–87
katydid, 98
killing, 87–88
lacewings, 109, 212
mantid flies, 109
mantis, preying, 46, 68, 224
metamorphosis of, 98
milkweed bug, 98
mounting on pins, 87–89
nets, 82
netting, 82
net-veined, 109
owl flies, 109
silverfish, 98
terrariums and cages for,
92–93
water insects, 94–95
woodland insects, 95

Insect strength, 114–18
  equipment for testing, 145
  feats of, 114

Kite, white-tailed, 69
Knots, 146–47
  bowline, 66

Lacewing flies, 212
Lichens, 161
Life histories, 95
Lines and ropes, 66, 146–47
  bowline slip-knot, 66
Lizard(s), 65–71
  anole, 65, 69–70
  chameleon, 65, 69
  chuckwallas, 69
  collared, 66, 70
  fence, 65, 70
  gecko, 65, 70
  gila monster, 65
  horned, 66, 70, 72
  leopard, 66, 70
  racerunner, 66
Lizard racetrack, 70–71

Mantis, preying, 46, 68, 224
Marten, 152, 153
Mazes, 77, 213
Mice, 162
Microscope, 156
Microscopic life, 156–60
Microscopic slides, preparing, 156
Moles, 162
Moths
  arctiids, 212
  catocala, 86
  dayflying, 86
  defenses of, against birds and
    bats, 46
  noctuids, 212

Neuroptera, 109

Opossums, 153
Owls
  barn, 23
  burrowing, 24
  great-horned, 14, 23
  saw-whet, 23
  screech, 23
  short-eared, 24
  stuffed, in tree, 50–51

Paramecium, 159, 177
Pinks, wild, 161
Plants, preserving, 224–25
Plant succession, 160–63
Pond life, 173–81

Rabbits, cottontail, 13
Rattlesnakes, 25, 60, 213
Ravens, 24
Ring-tailed cat, 20
Roadrunner, 24
Rotifers, 159, 177

Seashore animals, experiments
  with, 198–200
Seaweeds, collecting and
  mounting, 188–91
Seeds, spreading of, 162
Shrews, 162
Skunks, 15–18, 20
  tracks of, 146
Snakes, 57–62, 216–17, 219
  in captivity, 58–60
  garter, 61–62
  gopher, 24, 25, 59–60
  hog-nosed, 60–61
  king, 59, 62
  poisonous, 57–59, 213, 217

projects with, 62
racer, 59, 60, 62
rat, 59
rattlesnakes, 25, 60, 211
ring-necked, 61
rubber boa, 28
water, 59, 61
water moccasin, 216–17
whipsnake, 25, 60, 62
Sparrows, English, 34, 36
Spiders, 81, 119–40
arrow-shaped orb weaver, 130
black widow, 125
bowl and doily, 136
brown recluse, 125
circle-eyed grass, 130
domed orb-web, 132
extended legged, 134
filmy dome, 136
foliate, 130
garden, banded, 130
house, 130
jumping, 119–22
courtship of, 121
rearing young of, 122
testing jumps of, 120–21
labyrinth, 136
light-eyed, 134
losing fear of, 124
ogre-faced, 134
orb web weavers, 124, 130–31
photographing, 124–27
poisonous, 125
ray, 132–33
sheet web weavers, 130
six-eyed, 134
triangular, 123
violin, 125
webs, 123–35
white and dark-eyed, 134
Squirrels, 150–54
California ground, 153
feeding, 150
fox, 152
gray, 152
as hazards to birds, 35–36

red, 152
watching, 154
Starlings, 35–36
Succession of plants and animals,
155–63
Swamp life, exploring with
muskrat nest blind, 215–19
ducks, 217
equipment for, 216
grebe, pied-billed, 217
herons, 217
mink, 218
muskrats, 217–18
raccoons, 219
rice rats, 219
water moccasin, 217
Swamp life projects, 219

Tarantulas, 69
Temperature and humidity, 91
Terrariums, 66, 92–93, 95
pond and shore, 184–85
projects for, 184–85
Thermometers, wet and dry bulb,
91
Tide pools, 187–200
equipment for exploring,
187–88
life in, 194–97
photographing animals in,
191–94, 198
snorkel, 192
tide zones, 189
waterscopes, 192
Toads, spadefoot, 175–76
Tortoises, 76–78
Tracking and trail finding, 141–50
Tracks, 142–48
equipment for studying, 144
photographing, 145–48
projects for studying, 148
Traps, live
baits for, 169
black light, experiments with,
89–91

Traps, live (*continued*)
    black light, insect, 84–86,
        89–91
    ground, jars in, 82
    insect, 82
    jar and light, 95
    turtle, 75
Tree-dwelling animals, 151–54
Turtle maze, 77
Turtle race track, 78
Turtles and tortoises, 73–78
    box, 76
    loggerhead, 78
    musk, 77
    reaction to danger, 77
    sliders 73–74
    snapping, 75–76
    soft-shelled, 73, 75, 77

    stink-pot, 77–78
    terrapins, 75–76
    tortoises, 76
    wood turtles, 76

Vorticella, 159

Wasps, 68–69
Water boatmen, 212
Weasels, 20, 162, 208
Webs. *See* Spiders, webs
Wildcat, 14, 152, 153
Wild plant dealers, 235
Woodchuck, tracks of, 146
Worms, 162
    as meal, for lizards, 65